Birgit Walthall

Prime Time 8

Testen und Fördern

www.oebv.at

Liebe Schülerin, lieber Schüler!

Dieses Heft enthält **Tests** zu den Bereichen *Listening, Reading, Language in use* und *Writing*. Im Anschluss daran finden Sie Hinweise auf die jeweils überprüften **Kompetenzen** laut Gemeinsamem Europäischen Referenzrahmen für Sprachen (GERS) sowie **Förderhinweise** mit Verweisen auf passende Stellen in Ihrem *Coursebook*.

Die **Lösungen** finden Sie gesammelt am Ende des Buches.

Die Audio-Dateien, die Sie für die *Listening*-Aufgaben brauchen, finden Sie über einen

Online-Code auf der Website www.oebv.at.

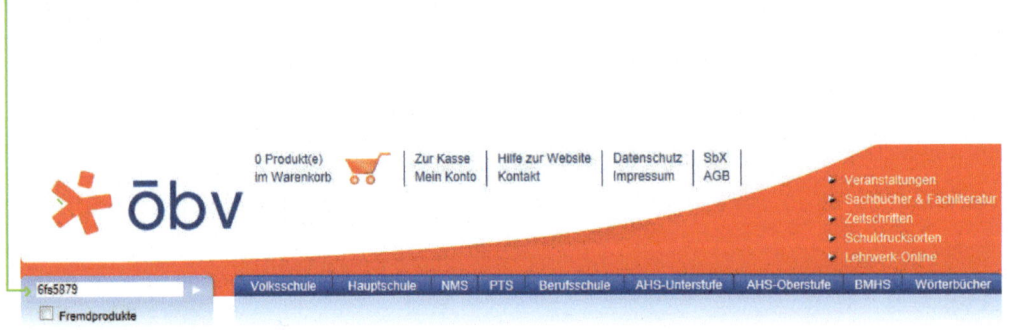

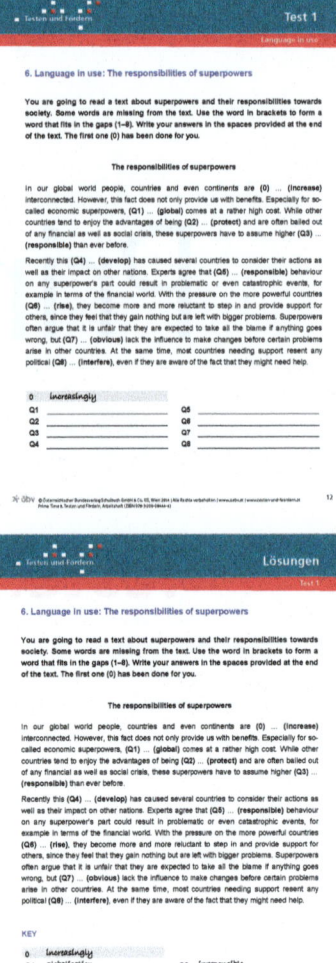

Hinweis für Lehrerinnen und Lehrer

Auf www.testen-und-foerdern.at finden Sie die abgedruckten Tests auch als Papiertests zum Download.

Weiters finden Sie dort Hinweise auf die jeweils überprüften **Kompetenzen** laut Gemeinsamem Europäischen Referenzrahmen für Sprachen (GERS) sowie Förderhinweise, die auf jeweils passende Stellen im *Coursebook* verweisen.

Nähere Informationen zum Onlineportal Testen-und-Fördern finden Sie auch auf www.oebv.at und auf www.testen-und-foerdern.at.

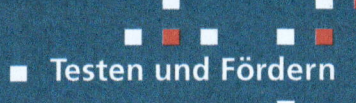

öbv © Österreichischer Bundesverlag Schulbuch GmbH & Co. KG, Wien 2014 | Alle Rechte vorbehalten | www.oebv.at | www.testen-und-foerdern.at
Prime Time 8. Testen und Fördern, Arbeitsheft (ISBN 978-3-209-08444-6)

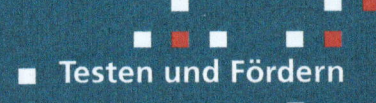 
1. Listening: Will boys still be boys?

You are going to listen to an interview about child development. First you will have 45 seconds to study the task below, then you will hear the recording twice. While listening, choose the correct answer (A, B, C or D) for questions 1–5. Put a ☒ in the correct box. The first one (0) has been done for you. After the second listening you will have 45 seconds to check your answers.

Will boys still be boys?

0 How often does "Modern Psychology" go on air?

   A once a day   ☐

   B once a week   ☒

   C once in two weeks   ☐

   D once a month   ☐

Q1 What was Dr Umbridge's main motivation to choose this line of work?

   A She was fascinated by the human mind.   ☐

   B She wanted to understand the functions of the human mind.   ☐

   C She wanted to help children express their anxieties.   ☐

   D She wanted to change children's life for the better.   ☐

Q2 Dr Umbridge's book points out that

   A boys cause more troubles growing up than girls.   ☐

   B parents expect more from boys than ever before.   ☐

   C mental disorders can be caused by negative experiences.   ☐

   D boys have problems in dealing with their current environment.   ☐

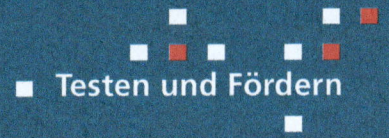

Q3 What does Dr Umbridge see as the main cause for the boys' problems?

A There has been an increase in the number of divorces. ☐

B Boys are confused about society's expectations. ☐

C There has been a change in societal and family conditions. ☐

D Boys feel put under pressure by their parents. ☐

Q4 According to Dr Umbridge, what tends to cause boys to develop OCDs?

A Their fathers force them to suppress their feelings. ☐

B One of their parents displays aggressive behavior. ☐

C They grow up in a family with very strict rules. ☐

D They do not know how to react to their parents' expectations. ☐

Q5 Why do boys struggle more with modern family structures than girls?

A They have to figure out their new place in society. ☐

B They need to accept a new set of values. ☐

C They prefer the traditional hierarchical family structures. ☐

D They are presented with higher expectations. ☐

  ōbv © Österreichischer Bundesverlag Schulbuch GmbH & Co. KG, Wien 2014 | Alle Rechte vorbehalten | www.oebv.at | www.testen-und-foerdern.at
Prime Time 8. Testen und Fördern, Arbeitsheft (ISBN 978-3-209-08444-6)

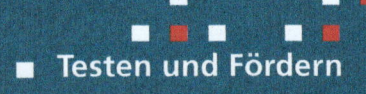

2. Listening: Are young Irish still traditional?

🔊 **You are going to listen to a recording about whether young Irish people are still interested in culture. First you will have 45 seconds to study the task below, then you will hear the recording twice. While listening, match the beginnings of the sentences (1–5) with the sentence endings (A–H). There are two extra sentence endings you should not use. Write your answers in the spaces provided. The first one (0) has been done for you. After the second listening you will have 45 seconds to check your answers.**

Are young Irish still traditional?

0	Roberta and Steven have agreed to …	E
Q1	The majority of the Irish are happy to …	
Q2	Teenagers in Ireland tend to …	
Q3	Irish humour is known to …	
Q4	Steven thinks that occasionally it is OK to …	
Q5	Irish teenagers have started to …	

A	… play a typical Irish instrument.
B	… express their pride in their culture.
C	… listen to Irish musicians.
D	… follow their families' traditions.
E	… participate in an interview about Irish culture.
F	… focus on a variety of forms.
G	… inquire more about their own culture.
H	… spread their culture.

✳ ōbv © Österreichischer Bundesverlag Schulbuch GmbH & Co. KG, Wien 2014 | Alle Rechte vorbehalten | www.oebv.at | www.testen-und-foerdern.at
Prime Time 8. Testen und Fördern, Arbeitsheft (ISBN 978-3-209-08444-6)

3. Reading: Trends in advertising

Read the text below, then complete the sentences (1–6) using a maximum of four words. Write your answers in the spaces provided. The first one (0) has been done for you.

Trends in advertising

Due to the pressure on businesses to increase their sales on the one hand and to reduce their costs on the other hand, the role of advertising in the media has become increasingly significant. While companies in former times relied mainly on televised advertisements, today the internet presents the biggest pool of possible customers.

Advertising has always been blamed for being rather stereotypical, since it usually displays quite unrealistic scenarios and images of perfect families, stunningly beautiful people and impossibly cute pets. The depiction of the real world is commonly not thought to be appealing enough to persuade customers to purchase certain products and to choose them over other rivalling brands.

Naturally, the way the two genders are portrayed in advertising has an enormous influence on how we perceive the products presented. Taking a closer look at the role of women in advertising, for example, it becomes obvious that certain types of women with specific characteristics appear more frequently than others.

Despite the fact that a few decades ago women were mainly cast for the role of a housewife, today advertisements tend to depict young, successful businesswomen, who are self-confident and independent. Younger audiences in particular appreciate the changes made, because they have an easier time to empathise with characters who try to achieve similar goals, such as professional success or personal well-being.

Due to these recent developments producers involved in the advertising business have also made changes to spots aimed at older target groups. These changes place an emphasis on how to enjoy a pleasant life after retirement and concentrate on products commonly not needed or used by younger viewers. Nevertheless, the spots produced do not portray the actors starring as elderly people who are approaching the end of their lives. On the contrary, a growing number of advertisements shows lively, athletic 60- to 70-year-olds who are only starting to realise how much they still want to achieve.

In addition, recent spots on TV are pleasantly lacking the formerly so strongly emphasised perfection. A strong tendency towards imperfection can be detected, which is a very different approach in comparison to former years. It almost seems as if the audience has

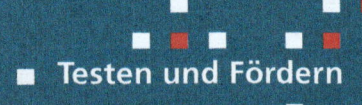
grown tired of being reminded what they themselves will most likely never have or be. More realistic advertisements provide us with a sense of comfort and satisfaction, because they leave us room to accept our own weaknesses and problems. Since the pressure of the modern world on all of us is steadily rising, it comes as no surprise that few viewers feel the desire to experience perfection in advertising.

However, the rules change when men form the main target group of a certain commercial. While women are perfectly happy to sympathise with imperfect female actors, men do not necessarily enjoy these new developments and expect to find certain stereotypes fulfilled in advertisements aiming at them. Thus, more and more production companies find themselves torn between meeting the expectations of modern women and still somewhat patriarchal men.

0	The most important medium for advertising is … .	*the internet*
Q1	People accuse advertisements of … .	
Q2	Too many references to reality might not lead to … .	
Q3	Recent adjustments in advertising especially appeal to … .	
Q4	The main focus of advertisements for older generations is on … .	
Q5	In former times, imperfection … .	
Q6	The gap in men's and women's ideas on advertising … .	

✶ ōbv © Österreichischer Bundesverlag Schulbuch GmbH & Co. KG, Wien 2014 | Alle Rechte vorbehalten | www.oebv.at | www.testen-und-foerdern.at
Prime Time 8. Testen und Fördern, Arbeitsheft (ISBN 978-3-209-08444-6)

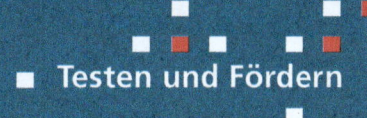

4. Reading: The challenges of going green

Read the text below, then decide whether the statements (1–7) are true (T) or false (F) and put a ⊠ in the correct box. Then identify the sentence in the text which supports your decision. Write the first four words of this sentence in the spaces provided. The first one (0) has been done for you.

The challenges of going green

After hundreds of years it seems that the human race has finally grasped that the planet's environment cannot continue to be corrupted any further. Already we suffer from the severe consequences, such as climate change, ozone layer depletion, extreme weather conditions, and destruction of the ocean's flora and fauna. However, this might only have been the start of a chain of events, if no action is taken to end this vicious circle of devastation.

These problems can mostly be traced back to an increase in energy consumption. The demand for all forms of energy, which has exploded over the past decade due to the rise of the world's population as well as its industry, has become almost impossible to meet for even the biggest energy corporations, due to the declining supply of natural resources. As a result, scientific research has focused on the development of alternative forms of energy production. The main problem lies in the fact that there is no consensus of which type of alternative solution should be favoured among scientists.

Among the various choices for clean energy production, three methods are most commonly used: wind, water, and solar energy. While in some cases the regional landscape and weather conditions are the determining factors, at other times economic aspects might influence the decision. Experts often opt for a combination of methods in order to secure energy supply at all times.

Even though several methods have been implemented and are being used successfully around the world, many governments are reluctant to rely on those solutions entirely. Apparently they fear economic drawbacks which might only show once large sums have been invested into these new industries. There is also no guarantee that investments made into alternative energies will produce the expected results. It might well be that seemingly promising methods produce less energy than consumed or prove to be less cost-efficient than thought. Additionally, turning back at this point might not be possible any more, which could result in the dependence of these governments on other states in matters of energy production.

ōbv © Österreichischer Bundesverlag Schulbuch GmbH & Co. KG, Wien 2014 | Alle Rechte vorbehalten | www.oebv.at | www.testen-und-foerdern.at
Prime Time 8. Testen und Fördern, Arbeitsheft (ISBN 978-3-209-08444-6)

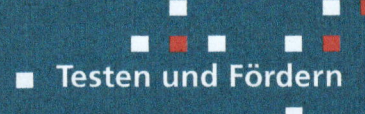
Apart from all those factors, the main challenge lies in making all of the parties involved understand the urgency of responding to the situation. Although the human race will still be able to rely on fossil fuels for some time, they will cease to be available to us at some point. The energy crisis is likely to become more and more of an issue, since resources will not be running out everywhere at the same time. Even in the best of cases scientists, governments, and energy corporations will have to cooperate for years to come up with suitable alternative solutions which can ultimately ensure the growing energy demand will be met. Failure to react now could easily result in a world-wide political and economic crisis.

As of now, there are small steps being taken to improve the current situation. In various countries governments are investing in the research of alternative energy and implement programmes aimed at reducing our negative impact on the environment. The sincerity with which these actions are taken will determine whether they will be successful and whether we can stop ourselves from going down a road that will ultimately lead to our ruin.

		Statement	T	F	Justification
0		Most people have understood that we cannot damage the environment any longer.	x		*After hundreds of years*
Q1		The problems we experience are very likely to have only been the beginning.			
Q2		Most energy corporations can no longer supply enough energy.			
Q3		Most scientists do not agree on which form of alternative energy is the best one.			
Q4		The location of a country influences its choice of energy production methods.			
Q5		Many countries refuse to use alternative forms of energy entirely.			
Q6		Countries using alternative forms of energy production might overestimate the success of these methods.			
Q7		Actions towards using alternative energy will have to be taken within the next few years to avoid severe consequences.			

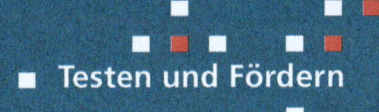
5. Language in use: Voluntary single

You are going to read a text about being single. In most lines of the text there is a word that should not be there. Write that word in the space provided after each line. Nine to eleven lines are correct. Indicate these lines with a tick (✓). There are two examples at the beginning.

Voluntary single

Text	Answer	Line
While magazines and books present our younger generations with an	✓	0
endless flood of information on how to find **out** the perfect partner, it	out	00
seems that many of young adults in their twenties are not even interested	___	Q1
in searching for the one to spend the rest of their lives with. They would	___	Q2
rather focus on their careers, enjoy the world to all the fullest, and	___	Q3
experience a phase of selfishness without having yet to consider the	___	Q4
feelings of another human being. After the desperate search conducted	___	Q5
by most generations before them, our youth seems to deal with this topic	___	Q6
in an incredibly relaxed way. So what is it that it has changed so much?	___	Q7
For one thing, society has become much more welcoming towards	___	Q8
single people. Entire businesses have focused on the new target	___	Q9
groups of voluntary singles, who have not only failed to find a partner, but	___	Q10
lead completely full and happy lives without one. Now that singles have	___	Q11
finally managed to get rid of the stigma of being socially incapable of,	___	Q12
especially women often enjoy the benefits being single can have in terms	___	Q13
of their professional careers. However, the question remains whether	___	Q14
these advantages come at too high a cost.	___	Q15

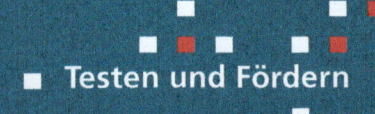
6. Language in use: The responsibilities of superpowers

You are going to read a text about superpowers and their responsibilities towards society. Some words are missing from the text. Use the word in brackets to form a word that fits in the gaps (1–8). Write your answers in the spaces provided at the end of the text. The first one (0) has been done for you.

The responsibilities of superpowers

In our global world people, countries and even continents are **(0)** … **(increase)** interconnected. However, this fact does not only provide us with benefits. Especially for so-called economic superpowers, **(Q1)** … **(global)** comes at a rather high cost. While other countries tend to enjoy the advantages of being **(Q2)** … **(protect)** and are often bailed out of any financial as well as social crisis, these superpowers have to assume higher **(Q3)** … **(responsible)** than ever before.

Recently this **(Q4)** … **(develop)** has caused several countries to consider their actions as well as their impact on other nations. Experts agree that **(Q5)** … **(responsible)** behaviour on any superpower's part could result in problematic or even catastrophic events, for example in terms of the financial world. With the pressure on the more powerful countries **(Q6)** … **(rise)**, they become more and more reluctant to step in and provide support for others, since they feel that they gain nothing but are left with bigger problems. Superpowers often argue that it is unfair that they are expected to take all the blame if anything goes wrong, but **(Q7)** … **(obvious)** lack the influence to make changes before certain problems arise in other countries. At the same time, most countries needing support resent any political **(Q8)** … **(interfere)**, even if they are aware of the fact that they might need help.

0	*increasingly*		
Q1	_____	Q5	_____
Q2	_____	Q6	_____
Q3	_____	Q7	_____
Q4	_____	Q8	_____

13

7. Writing: Studying abroad (Opinion essay)

"Studying abroad is the chance of a lifetime."

You are about to take your Matura and plan on studying afterwards. At university, there is the possibility to take part in exchange programmes which enable you to study in other countries for some time. Write an opinion essay, in which you either agree or disagree with the given statement.

- Outline reasons why students take/ do not take the chance to go abroad.
- Explain the impact of an exchange semester on your character development and social life.
- Discuss in how far your studies at home might be influenced by your decision.

Write an **opinion essay** of about **400 words**.

Fertigkeit	Task	Format	Themenbereich	GERS	Skills
Listening	Will boys still be boys?	MC	• Gedanken, Empfindungen und Gefühle • Umwelt und Gesellschaft	Kann im direkten Kontakt und in den Medien gesprochene Standardsprache verstehen, wenn es um vertraute oder auch um weniger vertraute Themen geht, wie man ihnen normalerweise im privaten, gesellschaftlichen, beruflichen Leben oder in der Ausbildung begegnet. Nur extreme Hintergrundgeräusche, unangemessene Diskursstrukturen oder starke Idiomatik beeinträchtigen das Verständnis.	Listening for specific information/important details; Listening for main ideas and supporting details
Listening	Are young Irish still interested in their culture?	MM	• Einstellungen und Werte • Umwelt und Gesellschaft	Kann die Hauptaussagen von inhaltlich und sprachlich komplexen Redebeiträgen zu konkreten und abstrakten Themen verstehen, wenn Standardsprache gesprochen wird; versteht auch Fachdiskussionen im eigenen Spezialgebiet. Kann längeren Redebeiträgen und komplexer Argumentation folgen, sofern die Thematik einigermaßen vertraut ist und der Rede- oder Gesprächsverlauf durch explizite Signale gekennzeichnet ist.	Listening for specific information/important details; Listening for main ideas and supporting details
Reading	The challenges of going green	TFJ	• Umwelt und Gesellschaft • Einstellungen und Werte	Kann sehr selbstständig lesen, Lesestil und -tempo verschiedenen Texten und Zwecken anpassen und geeignete Nachschlagewerke selektiv benutzen. Verfügt über einen großen Lesewortschatz, hat aber möglicherweise Schwierigkeiten mit seltener gebrauchten Wendungen.	Reading for specific information; Reading for important details; Reading for main ideas and supporting details

ED = Editing | MC = Multiple choice | MM = Multiple matching | NF = Note form | TFJ = True/False/Justification | WF = Word formation

Fertigkeit	Task	Format	Themenbereich	GERS	Skills
Reading	Trends in advertising	NF	• Umwelt und Gesellschaft • Einstellungen und Werte	Kann sehr selbstständig lesen, Lesestil und -tempo verschiedenen Texten und Zwecken anpassen und geeignete Nachschlagewerke selektiv benutzen. Verfügt über einen großen Lesewortschatz, hat aber möglicherweise Schwierigkeiten mit seltener gebrauchten Wendungen.	Reading for specific information; Reading for important details; Reading for main ideas and supporting details
LiU	Voluntary single	ED	• Einstellungen und Werte • Umwelt und Gesellschaft		
LiU	The responsibilities of superpowers	WF	• Umwelt und Gesellschaft • Interkulturelle und landeskundliche Aspekte		
Writing	Studying abroad	Essay	• Einstellungen und Werte • Umwelt und Gesellschaft • Schule und Arbeitswelt	Kann klare, detaillierte Texte zu verschiedenen Themen aus ihrem/seinem Interessengebiet verfassen und dabei Informationen und Argumente aus verschiedenen Quellen zusammenführen und gegeneinander abwägen.	

ED = Editing | MC = Multiple choice | MM = Multiple matching | NF = Note form | TFJ = True/False/Justification | WF = Word formation

Fertigkeit	Task	Format	Entsprechung in Schülerbuch Prime Time 8
Listening	Will boys still be boys?	MC	• A final peace (p. 9, ex. 1) – MC • Severn Suzuki's speech at the Summit (p. 24, ex. 2) – MC • Home is where the heart is (p. 53, ex. 1) – MC • A taboo topic (p. 84, ex. 2) – MC • I just want to do business (p. 108, ex. 3) – MC
Listening	Are young Irish still interested in their culture?	MM	• Saving the planet (p. 28, ex. 2) – MM • Migration (p. 48, ex. 4) – MM • The individual and society (p. 73, ex. 3) – MM • Science and technology (p. 99, ex. 1) – MM • Lifelong learning (p. 119, ex. 3) – MM
Reading	Trends in advertising	NF	• Saving the planet (p.22, ex. 1) – NF • Migration (p. 44, ex. 2) – NF • The individual and society (p. 68, ex. 2) – NF • Lifelong learning (p. 118, ex. 2) – NF • Lifelong learning (p. 124, ex. 2) – NF
Reading	The challenges of going green	TFJ	• Climate change takes its toll on Scotland (p. 29, ex. 3) – TFJ • Shopping madness (p. 82, ex. 2) – TFJ • At times I feel like a plastic Paki (p. 104, ex. 1) – TFJ

ED = Editing | MC = Multiple choice | MM = Multiple matching | NF = Note form | TFJ = True/False/Justification | WF = Word formation

ōbv © Österreichischer Bundesverlag Schulbuch GmbH & Co. KG, Wien 2014 | Alle Rechte vorbehalten | www.oebv.at | www.testen-und-foerdern.at
Prime Time 8. Testen und Fördern, Arbeitsheft (ISBN 978-3-209-08444-6)

Fertigkeit	Task	Format	Entsprechung in Schülerbuch Prime Time 8
LiU	Voluntary single	ED	• Mars (p. 17, ex. 3) – ED • Editing (p. 65, ex. 3) – ED • Brightworks (p. 125, ex. 4) – ED
LiU	The responsibilities of superpowers	WF	• The future of green America (p. 27, ex. 3) – WF • Canada: New pioneers (p. 52, ex. 2) – WF • Word formation (p. 86, ex. 2) – WF

ED = Editing | MC = Multiple choice | MM = Multiple matching | NF = Note form | TFJ = True/False/Justification | WF = Word formation

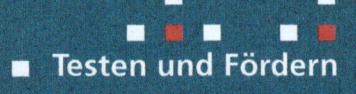
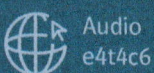
1. Listening: What did you learn today?

🔊 **You are going to listen to an interview about learning abilities. First you will have 45 seconds to study the task below, then you will hear the recording twice. While listening, complete the sentences (1–6) using a maximum of four words. Write your answers in the spaces provided. The first one (0) has been done for you. After the second listening you will have 45 seconds to check your answers.**

What did you learn today?

0	"Amazing News" focuses on … .	*current topics and developments*
Q1	At Coleman's Institute Dr Scott's field of duty is to … .	
Q2	In the future our brain might be able to learn … .	
Q3	In order to find out about people's learning capabilities, the researchers … .	
Q4	When we learn, we combine smaller, individual units to … .	
Q5	… presents the biggest danger to our ability to learn.	
Q6	Our brain can deal with changes in our surroundings, because it … .	

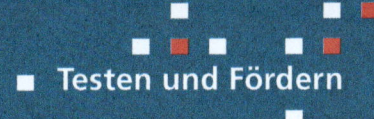

19

2. Listening: Dealing with money

You are going to listen to a discussion between mother and daughter about plastic money. First you will have 45 seconds to study the task below, then you will hear the recording twice. While listening, answer the questions (1–5) using a maximum of four words. Write your answers in the spaces provided. The first one (0) has been done for you. After the second listening you will have 45 seconds to check your answers.

Dealing with money

0	What is the mother complaining about?	*daughter spending money*
Q1	What is meant by "living in medieval times"?	
Q2	Which option do credit cards offer?	
Q3	What happens when the entire credit card bill isn't paid off?	
Q4	What is the biggest danger in others obtaining your bank account information?	
Q5	How do reliable companies protect their customers?	

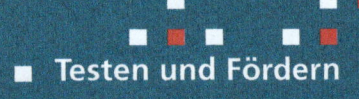
3. Reading: Why scientists could easily be ruling the world

Read the text below, then choose the correct answer (A, B, C or D) for questions 1–5. Put a ⊠ in the correct box. The first one (0) has been done for you.

Why scientists could easily be ruling the world

Abortion is an extremely controversial topic in the United States with both sides of the debate duelling it out over what is right or wrong. The law presently controlling abortion in America was introduced in 1973 by the Supreme Court. According to this law, women have the right to choose how they want to handle a pregnancy, whether through termination or continuation. Since this court ruling, abortion has been in the national spotlight and the centre of the debate still remains whether it should actually still be legal or overturned.

Before this ruling there had been abortion laws in the US as early as the 1820s. However, by 1900 most abortions had been outlawed because of the extreme pressure from the American Medical Association, physicians and legislators. Nevertheless, this did not prevent illegal abortions, which at the time were a dangerous practice, from taking place. The main difference was that women did not only risk their lives due to the bad hygienic conditions under which such procedures took place, but also because few abortions were carried out by medical professionals any more. By 1965, all states had banned abortions altogether, with few exceptions being allowed. Finally, abortion was once again legalised in 1973 in all fifty states, using a trimester framework that freed doctors to perform abortions for any reason in the first trimester and giving the individual states the power to regulate the second and third trimester. In the years since this decision many pro-life groups, such as the Human Life Foundation or the Life Coalition, have been formed which have taken up the fight against this ruling and presented alternatives such as adoption. They have been the driving forces behind new restrictions and regulations that have been introduced, such as required parental consent for teenagers. These pro-life organisations arrange many protests and lobby to bring forth legislation to end the age-old debate of how to handle an unexpected pregnancy. Often, these groups see the practice of abortion as an unlawful procedure that takes a defenseless human life and advocate adoption as the only legal alternative. Furthermore, they argue that life begins at conception, whereas the other side

20

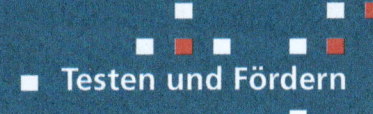
of the debate believes that no rights other than those stated in the Constitution should be judicially recognised and protected.

There are many different reasons why a woman might decide to have an abortion. If there are irreparable defects concerning the fetus, such as major development failures or problems with the heart, nervous system, brain, kidneys or breathing system, a woman might choose to end the pregnancy. There are other common reasons that a woman might choose to have an abortion such as birth control failure, unwanted or unplanned pregnancy, not being able to support or provide for the child or medical conditions that could seriously endanger the woman's health. Most women concerned choose to abort based on their current needs, feelings and economic position. Especially women aged between 15 and 20 often do not feel prepared to take responsibility for another human being. They might lack sufficient means to provide for themselves and a child. Unfinished education and lack of mental maturity are factors that particularly cause young females to abort. However, younger women are not the only ones making such drastic decisions, which may have a strong impact on their future lives. Research shows that abortions are no longer limited to a certain age group of women.

On average, one million women in the US decide to abort their unborn children every year. This decision, which is often made in a moment of desperation or panic, may cause inner turmoil and stress. No matter whether having an abortion is legal or not, in the end it is always the woman who has to deal with the choice she has made.

ōbv © Österreichischer Bundesverlag Schulbuch GmbH & Co. KG, Wien 2014 | Alle Rechte vorbehalten | www.oebv.at | www.testen-und-foerdern.at
Prime Time 8. Testen und Fördern, Arbeitsheft (ISBN 978-3-209-08444-6)

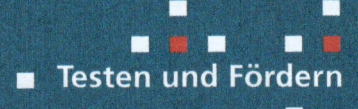
0 The 1973 law

    A banned abortion. ☐

    B legalised abortion. ☒

    C led to a protest. ☐

    D was overturned. ☐

Q1 Banning abortion around 1900 caused

    A a lot of pressure from doctors and lawyers. ☐

    B an increase in death following abortion. ☐

    C a rise in the practice of illegal abortion. ☐

    D a decrease of medical professionals. ☐

Q2 Regulations on abortion after 1973

    A allowed abortion up to the second trimester. ☐

    B allowed abortion throughout the US. ☐

    C banned abortion after the second trimester. ☐

    D banned abortion in individual states. ☐

Q3 The formation of pro-life groups resulted in

    A stronger support for single mothers. ☐

    B the creation of educational programmes. ☐

    C stricter regulations on abortion. ☐

    D a ban on teenage abortion. ☐

Q4 The main reason for teenage girls to abort is their

    A psychological stability. ☐

    B physical maturity. ☐

    C financial situation. ☐

    D educational background. ☐

Q5 What is the purpose of the text?

    A to criticise women who abort ☐

    B to illustrate the dangers of abortion ☐

    C to argue a ban on abortion ☐

    D to explain the background of abortion ☐

✱ ōbv © Österreichischer Bundesverlag Schulbuch GmbH & Co. KG, Wien 2014 | Alle Rechte vorbehalten | www.oebv.at | www.testen-und-foerdern.at
Prime Time 8. Testen und Fördern, Arbeitsheft (ISBN 978-3-209-08444-6)

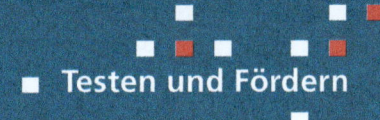
4. Reading: The newspaper of the future

Read the text below. Parts of the text have been removed. Choose the correct part (A–I) for the gaps (1–6). There are two extra parts you should not use. Write your answers in the boxes provided. The first one (0) has been done for you.

The newspaper of the future

Ever since the invention of printing methods effective enough to **(0)** ... , a printed version of the latest news has been a consistent and reliable part of our lives. We even got used to **(Q1)** ... and to be aware as well as warned of right to our front door, ever since a system for subscription and delivery was introduced.

For a few years now, however, it seemed as if this precious part of our society was on a fast decrease, due to its own reinvention on the internet. People aged between 15 and 30 in particular admit to **(Q2)** ... to all kinds of news online and even point out the benefit of being able to compare and contrast different sources before making up their mind about certain events. Furthermore, appealing features such as live feeds and supporting video material add to the belief that online newspapers present the reader with a much more wholesome picture of what is happening around the globe than traditional papers ever could.

So why should we even mourn the slow death of the traditional newspaper? In terms of immediate accessibility, faster spreading of current events and availability of further information it seems at a clear disadvantage when **(Q3)** ... . It is also more costly, more prone to being impacted by catastrophic events due to possible difficulties in production, and much less extensive in terms of the information it provides. There are, however, quite a few points **(Q4)** ... .

While online versions claim their vast amount of information as a benefit, readers can easily be overwhelmed by the sheer number of articles available to them on certain topics. They might become side-tracked and actually restrict their own view because they rarely take the time to sort through all the topics of the day. Thus, online readers tend to focus on specific areas of interest but neglect even skimming over anything else. This is made possible because every online version contains a search link **(Q5)** ... where they want to go.

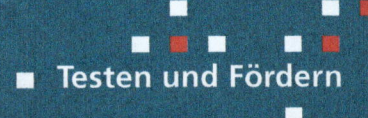
Due to the speed news are spreading with, online papers can easily become a perfect platform for exaggeration as well as hysteria and consequently the source of panic among the masses. Even smaller events which might not have been **(Q6)** ... a few decades back now lead to lengthy discussions and unnecessary fear among citizens. While there are quite a few beneficial aspects to the reduction in time news need to spread, such as quicker responses of rescue teams and charity organisations to disasters or catastrophes, there are obviously also drawbacks to this development.

Nevertheless, latest trends point towards new and improved combinations of both, printed as well as online newspapers, which might enable future readers to enjoy the best of both worlds.

A	relying entirely on having access
B	introduced to the audience
C	compared to online versions
D	explaining the disadvantage of newspapers
E	produce books and newspaper for the masses
F	taken all that seriously
G	defending the importance of the traditional newspaper
H	having all we ever needed to know
I	enabling the audience to get directly to

0	Q1	Q2	Q3	Q4	Q5	Q6
E						

öbv © Österreichischer Bundesverlag Schulbuch GmbH & Co. KG, Wien 2014 | Alle Rechte vorbehalten | www.oebv.at | www.testen-und-foerdern.at
Prime Time 8. Testen und Fördern, Arbeitsheft (ISBN 978-3-209-08444-6)

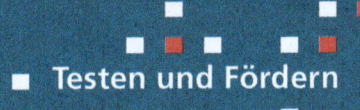
5. Language in use: Should more fathers be spending time with their children?

You are going to read a text about men staying at home with their children. Some words are missing from the text. Choose from the list (A–N) the correct part for each gap (1–11) in the text. There are two extra words you should not use. Write your answers in the boxes provided. The first one (0) has been done for you.

Should more fathers be spending time with their children?

The current discussion **(0)** ... around why fathers are often still very reluctant to be a stay-at-home dad has shown that most of them feel that their profession does not **(Q1)** ... for such a decision. Even though over 50 per cent of men claimed that they would like to have the possibility of **(Q2)** ... their children for some time, very few fathers take the actual step. In many cases they feel intimidated due to the doubts being **(Q3)** ... by their work environment if they will be able to juggle their career while **(Q4)** ... up their children at the same time. Although mothers have been **(Q5)** ... with the very same problem for decades, the world does not seem to be entirely ready for fathers to take on this new role. Apart from the fact that many companies are not yet **(Q6)** ... with child care facilities and much less offer proper part-time employment opportunities, there are still strong tendencies in society towards **(Q7)** ... the mother as the proper caretaker of a small child.

Nevertheless, laws have been **(Q8)** ... by many governments which **(Q9)** ... both partners to equally share the time they spend with their children. Therefore, the main problem seems to lie in the fact that men often **(Q10)** ... ridicule by their peers should they decide to **(Q11)** ... their children over their careers.

A allow	**E** equipped	**I** passed	**M** struggling
B bringing	**F** expressed	**J** raising	**N** viewing
C choose	**G** face	~~**K** revolving~~	
D enable	**H** invented	**L** rising	

0	Q1	Q2	Q3	Q4	Q5	Q6	Q7	Q8	Q9	Q10	Q11
K											

✳ ōbv © Österreichischer Bundesverlag Schulbuch GmbH & Co. KG, Wien 2014 | Alle Rechte vorbehalten | www.oebv.at | www.testen-und-foerdern.at
Prime Time 8. Testen und Fördern, Arbeitsheft (ISBN 978-3-209-08444-6)

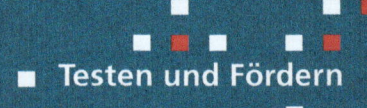
6. Language in use: Going virtual

You are going to read a text about virtual life. Some words are missing from the text. Choose the correct answer (A, B, C or D) for each gap (1–7) in the text. Write your answers in the boxes provided. The first one (0) has been done for you.

Going virtual

(0) ... studies have shown that there might be numerous benefits to spending time in a virtual world, provided that the person **(Q1)** ... does not lose touch with reality. Experts in brain development **(Q2)** ... have discovered that people deal better with many real-life scenarios if they have gone over them in their minds repeatedly. Thus, spending some time in a virtual reality could result in an increase in a person's actual **(Q3)** ... , such as better sportsmanship or improved social skills.

Thus, psychiatrists as well as therapists have started to reap the **(Q4)** ... of the multitude of available scenarios the virtual world offers. Their patients can face fears and phobias, while knowing that they are perfectly safe and therefore practice taking different **(Q5)** ... to problematic situations. The more frequently they are introduced to such forms of therapy, the more comfortable they become with similar situations in real life.

Furthermore, this technology has been adopted by universities and other educational institutions in order to prepare their students for worldly scenarios they will **(Q6)** ... in their professional lives. This includes business meetings, giving speeches in front of crowds, conflict management, and negotiations. By **(Q7)** ... their students with in-depth training, schools believe that they can ensure a more capable and efficient generation of future employees or employers.

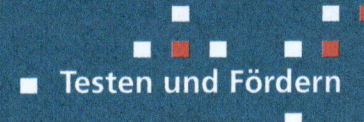
| 0 | A | Recent | B | Latest | C | Modern | D | Contemporary |

| **0** | ~~**A**~~ | Recent | **B** | Latest | **C** | Modern | **D** | Contemporary |

Q1 **A** involved   **B** convoluted   **C** affected   **D** concerned

Q2 **A** study   **B** research   **C** investigation   **D** exploration

Q3 **A** abilities   **B** facilities   **C** aptitudes   **D** capacities

Q4 **A** aids   **B** paybacks   **C** benefits   **D** assistances

Q5 **A** tactics   **B** approaches   **C** attitudes   **D** methods

Q6 **A** come upon   **B** bump into   **C** struggle   **D** encounter

Q7 **A** offering   **B** showing   **C** providing   **D** obtaining

0	**Q1**	**Q2**	**Q3**	**Q4**	**Q5**	**Q6**	**Q7**
A							

öbv © Österreichischer Bundesverlag Schulbuch GmbH & Co. KG, Wien 2014 | Alle Rechte vorbehalten | www.oebv.at | www.testen-und-foerdern.at
Prime Time 8. Testen und Fördern, Arbeitsheft (ISBN 978-3-209-08444-6)

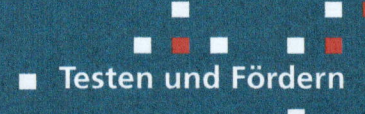
7. Writing: Online shopping (Report)

Over the last few English lessons you have heard a lot about the increase in online stores and online shopping. Your English teacher has asked you to write a **report**, in which you describe several aspects of shopping over the internet. In your report, you should:

- outline the importance of online shopping for people today
- describe advantages and dangers of shopping over the internet
- recommend safe ways to shop online

Write a **report** of about **250 words**. Divide your report into **sections** and give them **headings**.

28

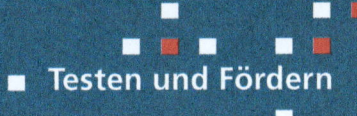
Fertigkeit	Task	Format	Themenbereich	GERS	Skills
Listening	What did you learn today?	NF	• Umwelt und Gesellschaft • Schule und Arbeitswelt	Kann im direkten Kontakt und in den Medien gesprochene Standardsprache verstehen, wenn es um vertraute oder auch um weniger vertraute Themen geht, wie man ihnen normalerweise im privaten, gesellschaftlichen, beruflichen Leben oder in der Ausbildung begegnet. Nur extreme Hintergrundgeräusche, unangemessene Diskursstrukturen oder starke Idiomatik beeinträchtigen das Verständnis.	Listening for specific information/important details; Listening for main ideas and supporting details
Listening	Dealing with money	NFQ	• Einstellungen und Werte • Umwelt und Gesellschaft • Kindheit und Erwachsen-werden	Kann im direkten Kontakt und in den Medien gesprochene Standardsprache verstehen, wenn es um vertraute oder auch um weniger vertraute Themen geht, wie man ihnen normalerweise im privaten, gesellschaftlichen, beruflichen Leben oder in der Ausbildung begegnet. Nur extreme Hintergrundgeräusche, unangemessene Diskursstrukturen oder starke Idiomatik beeinträchtigen das Verständnis.	Listening for specific information/important details; Listening for main ideas and supporting details
Reading	Why scientists could easily be ruling the world	MC	• Umwelt und Gesellschaft • Einstellungen und Werte	Kann sehr selbstständig lesen, Lesestil und -tempo verschiedenen Texten und Zwecken anpassen und geeignete Nachschlagewerke selektiv benutzen. Verfügt über einen großen Lesewortschatz, hat aber möglicherweise Schwierigkeiten mit seltener gebrauchten Wendungen.	Reading for specific information; Reading for important details; Reading for main ideas and supporting details

BGF = Banked gap fill | MC = Multiple choice | MM = Multiple matching | NF = Note form | NFQ = Note form with questions

Fertigkeit	Task	Format	Themenbereich	GERS	Skills
Reading	The newspaper of the future	MM	• Umwelt und Gesellschaft • Einstellungen und Werte • Kultur, Medien und Literatur	Kann sehr selbstständig lesen, Lesestil und -tempo verschiedenen Texten und Zwecken anpassen und geeignete Nachschlagewerke selektiv benutzen. Verfügt über einen großen Lesewortschatz, hat aber möglicherweise Schwierigkeiten mit seltener gebrauchten Wendungen.	Reading for specific information; Reading for important details; Reading for main ideas and supporting details
LiU	Should more fathers be spending time with their children?	BGF	• Umwelt und Gesellschaft • Kindheit und Erwachsen-werden • Gedanken, Empfindungen und Gefühle		
LiU	Going virtual	MC	• Einstellungen und Werte • Umwelt und Gesellschaft • Kultur, Medien und Literatur		
Writing	Online shopping	Report	• Einstellungen und Werte • Umwelt und Gesellschaft • Kultur, Medien und Literatur	Kann klare, detaillierte Texte zu verschiedenen Themen aus ihrem/seinem Interessengebiet verfassen und dabei Informationen und Argumente aus verschiedenen Quellen zusammenführen und gegeneinander abwägen.	

BGF = Banked gap fill | MC = Multiple choice | MM = Multiple matching | NF = Note form | NFQ = Note form with questions

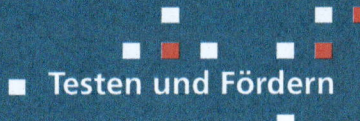
Fertigkeit	Task	Format	Entsprechung in Schülerbuch Prime Time 8
Listening	What did you learn today?	NF	• One world (p. 56, ex. 2) – NF • Big money (p. 88, ex. 1) – NF • Ideals and reality (p. 113, ex. 2) – NF
Listening	Dealing with money	NFQ	• Gender issues (p. 37, ex. 3) - NFQ
Reading	Why scientists could easily be ruling the world	MC	• Gender issues (p. 32, ex. 1) – MC • One world (p. 64, ex. 2) – MC • Science and technology (p. 94, ex. 2) – MC
Reading	The newspaper of the future	MM	• Ireland (p. 16, ex. 1) – MM • Migration (p. 50, ex. 1) – MM • One world (p. 58, ex. 2) – MM • The individual and society (p. 70, ex. 2) – MM • The individual and society (p. 75, ex. 1) – MM • Ideals and reality (p. 112, ex. 1) – MM

BGF = Banked gap fill | MC = Multiple choice | MM = Multiple matching | NF = Note form | NFQ = Note form with questions

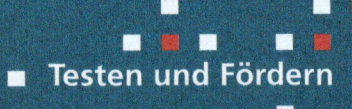
Fertigkeit	Task	Format	Entsprechung in Schülerbuch Prime Time 8
LiU	Should more fathers be spending time with their children?	BGF	• Green shopping (p. 26, ex. 1) – MC • Formal English (p. 62, ex. 1) – MC • Cyber Monday tips for safe online shopping (p. 89, ex. 3) – MC • Stem cells (p. 101, ex. 4) – MC
LiU	Going virtual	MC	• Choosing the right register (p. 62, ex. 2) – BGF • The word "get" in formal English (p. 77, ex. 3) – BGF • Marketers target kids with technology (p. 87, ex. 3) – BGF

BGF = Banked gap fill | MC = Multiple choice | MM = Multiple matching | NF = Note form | NFQ = Note form with questions

⋇ ōbv   © Österreichischer Bundesverlag Schulbuch GmbH & Co. KG, Wien 2014 | Alle Rechte vorbehalten | www.oebv.at | www.testen-und-foerdern.at
Prime Time 8. Testen und Fördern, Arbeitsheft (ISBN 978-3-209-08444-6)

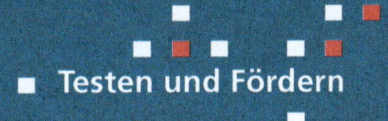
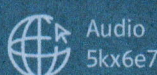
1. Listening: The conflict of individualism

You are going to listen to an interview about the conflict of individualism. First you will have 45 seconds to study the task below, then you will hear the recording twice. While listening, choose the correct answer (A, B, C or D) for questions 1–5. Put a ☒ in the correct box. The first one (0) has been done for you. After the second listening you will have 45 seconds to check your answers.

The conflict of individualism

0 How often does this radio show air?

A every week   ☐

B every two weeks   ☒

C twice a week   ☐

D once a month   ☐

Q1 Mr Janks' interest in the topic was raised by

A the enormous changes he observed.   ☐

B the widening gap between society and individual.   ☐

C the growing freedom of individuals.   ☐

D the implications of an increase in individualism.   ☐

Q2 What did the term "individualism" express in former times?

A the ability to go beyond society's limits   ☐

B the individual's functions in society   ☐

C the perception of our private lives   ☐

D the difference between people in society and as an individual   ☐

ōbv © Österreichischer Bundesverlag Schulbuch GmbH & Co. KG, Wien 2014 | Alle Rechte vorbehalten | www.oebv.at | www.testen-und-foerdern.at
Prime Time 8. Testen und Fördern, Arbeitsheft (ISBN 978-3-209-08444-6)

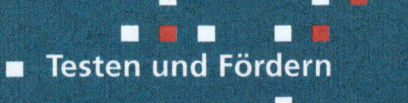

Q3 What is problematic about the newly evolving form of "individualism"?

A Responsibility towards society ceases to exist. ☐

B Unacceptable behaviour occurs among individualists. ☐

C Individualism becomes a private lifestyle. ☐

D Individualism interferes with our social duties. ☐

Q4 Recent developments around the world point towards

A a lack of responsibility towards other ☐

B a rise in the number of individualists ☐

C an increase in criminal activity ☐

D a decrease in recklessness among individualists ☐

Q5 According to Mr Janks, what danger are we already facing?

A falling into anarchy ☐

B loss of all established rules ☐

C destruction of society ☐

D irreversible consequences ☐

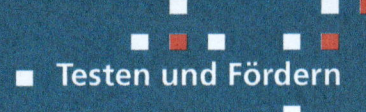

2. Listening: Does globalisation threaten our national identity?

You are going to listen to an interview about globalisation and national identity. First you will have 45 seconds to study the task below, then you will hear the recording twice. While listening, complete the sentences (1–6) using a maximum of four words. Write your answers in the spaces provided. The first one (0) has been done for you. After the second listening you will have 45 seconds to check your answers.

Does globalisation threaten our national identity?

0	Professor Storms is an expert on	*globalisation and its effects*
Q1	After working for a multinational company, Professor Storms returned to	
Q2	Personal identities remain stagnant except for the occurrence of	
Q3	People's national identities ... their personal identities.	
Q4	Global factors have an influence on how	
Q5	Protest among citizens is usually caused by	
Q6	Citizens are less supportive of countries which make use of	

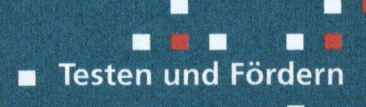
3. Reading: The misery of illegal aliens

Read the text below, then choose the correct answer (A, B, C or D) for questions 1–5. Put a 🗵 in the correct box. The first one (0) has been done for you.

The misery of illegal aliens

Ever since the gap between industrialised and developing countries has become so wide, there has been an increase in illegal immigration into the countries that are economically better off. It could be argued that travelling to or staying in another state illegally is a mistake to begin with, since it leaves the immigrants with a lot of problems. However, thousands of people have little to no chance to be accepted as a legal immigrant or to be given a visa for economic reasons. This forces many of them to use alternative ways which might be illegal, but at least seems to provide them with the chance to achieve their ultimate goal of leaving their home country and settling down in a country which might offer a job and even a small, regular income.

Apart from the seemingly ample benefits, many so-called illegal aliens face a whole myriad of problems once they arrive at their destination. Not only do they live in fear of being discovered and deported back to their country of origin, in the most extreme cases there is even the danger of being imprisoned. Reoccurring illegal migrating activities may lead to serious legal charges. Furthermore, on a daily basis there are all kinds of difficulties, especially when dealing with the authorities.

Unlike normal citizens, illegal immigrants have trouble obtaining any type of legal document or performing legal actions, such as getting a local driver's licence or registering a car in their name. Since they do not exist in a legal sense, small obstacles in their way towards a better existence and standard of living can easily become insurmountable difficulties. Another very real consequence of having no permit to stay in a country is the fact that illegal aliens are often subject to exploitation.

Due to their problematic status, there is little to no protection against people who are trying to use illegal immigrants to their own advantage. If they manage to find accommodation, for example, there is no guarantee that the landlord will treat them in a fair way. They might be thrown out without a warning or be forced to pay much higher rent than usual. Although local people often argue that the problem lies in the language barrier or the difference in culture, the underlying fact is a different one. Illegal immigrants are dependent on the mercy of other people and have no possibility to take any legal action towards people who exploit them or treat them inappropriately.

Apart from possible mistreatment, there is another major drawback to crossing boarders illegally. After their initial arrival many illegal immigrants become aware of the fact that they

❋ ōbv   © Österreichischer Bundesverlag Schulbuch GmbH & Co. KG, Wien 2014 | Alle Rechte vorbehalten | www.oebv.at | www.testen-und-foerdern.at
Prime Time 8. Testen und Fördern, Arbeitsheft (ISBN 978-3-209-08444-6)

might have robbed themselves of any way to ever return to their home country in a legal way. The reason for that is the problem of obtaining a permit to stay once you have entered the country illegally. Most countries are determined to withhold such benefits from persons who never had an official permission to immigrate, which prevents many illegal immigrants from applying for a visa in the first place. Thus, illegal immigrants might never be able to leave their chosen destination again. Without proof of being a legal immigrant, they would be stopped at the boarder or at any airport when trying to travel and would be taken in for questioning. Most likely they would never be allowed to return after facing the usual consequence of being deported back to their home country. Since most people refrain from facing such a risk, they do not travel outside of their new home country.

Finally, employment and health care are also very problematic for those people. Naturally, nobody will be able to employ them officially, so they are stuck with low-skill jobs that are commonly badly paid. Most well-paid jobs require legal documents and proof of education, which are hard to get in this situation. Without a working permit, however, there will be no health benefits that typically come with a stable job. Since the majority of people do not make enough money to afford private insurance, this usually results in little or no health care. Living ever day in fear of falling ill is reality for many illegal immigrants.

0 Illegal immigration is high in countries which

    A offer better economic circumstances.   ☒

    B are developing into rich nations.   ☐

    C are politically rather stable.   ☐

    D offer easy ways of immigration.   ☐

Q1 Most of these immigrants make the decision to do so illegally, because

    A they have no income in their home country.   ☐

    B they expect a higher living standard.   ☐

    C they have run out of alternative ways.   ☐

    D they believe they have no legal chance.   ☐

Q2 Illegal immigrants may be put into jail, if

    A they are to be deported back to their country of origin. ☐

    B they are found to immigrate without permission repeatedly. ☐

    C they are forced to deal with the authorities ☐

    D they are involved in other criminal activities. ☐

Q3 Because of their illegal situation, many immigrants

    A lose their driver's licence. ☐

    B cannot buy a new car. ☐

    C depend on other people's trust. ☐

    D cannot get a new passport. ☐

Q4 Often such immigrants run into problems with landlords, because

    A they cannot pay the rent. ☐

    B they do not speak the local language. ☐

    C they cannot take others to court. ☐

    D they misunderstand the local culture. ☐

Q5 Illegal immigrants' fear to apply for an official visa is caused by

    A the government's refusal to grant them. ☐

    B the restrictions on travelling back home. ☐

    C the threat of deportation through boarder control. ☐

    D the costs for such an official document. ☐

öbv © Österreichischer Bundesverlag Schulbuch GmbH & Co. KG, Wien 2014 | Alle Rechte vorbehalten | www.oebv.at | www.testen-und-foerdern.at
Prime Time 8. Testen und Fördern, Arbeitsheft (ISBN 978-3-209-08444-6)

4. Reading: Peace – Mission Impossible?

Read the text below, then answer the questions (1–6) using a maximum of four words. Write your answers in the spaces provided. The first one (0) has been done for you.

Peace – Mission Impossible?

Although the world has seen two World Wars and suffered the consequences of such major events, humankind appears to have learned little about how to live in peace with each other. There are still many unresolved conflicts with the potential of drawing many other countries into them as well. Due to alliances and organisations binding several countries together, political statements and actions have to be watched closely, since they might not only trigger the reaction of the country attacked or insulted, but also of several others.

Nevertheless, many wars in the past have taught us some important lessons about the extreme losses resulting from military conflicts. We can still vividly remember pictures of destroyed buildings, injured or dead soldiers as well as civilians, and half-starved children. It is usually the normal population who suffer most from wars. Apart from the fact that many fall victim to attacks, the economy of the country concerned often comes to a screeching halt. This results in high unemployment rates, inflation and lack of resources, such as food or energy. In addition, it can take the economy years to recover from the decrease in industry and production as well as the destruction of infrastructure.

With all those factors in mind, it seems to be obvious that keeping peace should be the top priority of any government. Not only are there extensive economic benefits, since multinational companies tend to choose peaceful countries as headquarters and to run main operations in, but there is first and foremost a climate of political stability. People who live in peaceful times tend to appreciate their government and politicians more and are also willing to support the political system they live in. In addition, they are more productive, because they profit from their own hard work and manage to establish a higher standard of living.

Thus, the questions remains, why countries decide against peace, if there are so many clear advantages to it. One determining factor why countries enter into military conflict is political reasons. In cases where the population is suppressed by a military regime or a dictatorship, other countries might decide to spring into action in order to enforce a more stable system. Whether this is the right way to deal with such situations is questionable. Especially when a country suffers from civil war, soldiers from other countries are often sent in to stop the violence. On the other hand, frequent violations of human rights through governments such as torture, censorship or unjustified imprisonment are also often the cause for arising conflicts, which are usually following an international outcry.

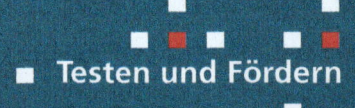
Nevertheless, the main problem with an ideal world living in peace lies in the character of human beings. Although we possess a certain control over our feelings, aggression is still among our basic instinctive reactions. Whenever we feel insulted or attacked, our initial urge goes towards using violence for protection and defence. Even though we realise that this desire might be misplaced and might not go through with it, keeping the peace might be more difficult for us than one might hope.

0	What threatens peace today?	Unresolved conflicts
Q1	Who might react to political insults or activities?	
Q2	In terms of financial matters, what do wars often result in?	
Q3	What has to be increased in order to reverse the effects of war?	
Q4	What is the main benefit of peace?	
Q5	According to the author, what reason might rightfully cause a conflict?	
Q6	How do people react to provocation?	

öbv © Österreichischer Bundesverlag Schulbuch GmbH & Co. KG, Wien 2014 | Alle Rechte vorbehalten | www.oebv.at | www.testen-und-foerdern.at
Prime Time 8. Testen und Fördern, Arbeitsheft (ISBN 978-3-209-08444-6)

5. Language in use: Do our own needs surpass our compassion for others?

You are going to read a text about needs. Some words are missing from the text. Use the word in brackets to complete each gap (1–9). Write your answers in the spaces provided at the end of the text. The first one (0) has been done for you.

Do our own needs surpass our compassion for others?

Unlike centuries ago, the **(0)** ... **(major)** of people in our society today enjoy a life where their most basic needs, such as a place to live, food and medical **(Q1)** ... **(treat)** are covered. Due to the quite extensive **(Q2)** ... **(safe)** net most western states offer, even people in potentially **(Q3)** ... **(economy)** difficult situations such as **(Q4)** ... **(employ)**, or health problems are usually provided with enough financial means to live on. As a consequence, our priorities in terms of desires seem to have shifted. The more security we have in life, the more **(Q5)** ... **(focus)** we become on more elaborate desires, such as a successful professional life, or happy personal relationships.

However, in recent years our personal needs tend to emphasise our desire to develop our **(Q6)** ... **(personal)** as well as to evaluate our own progress. First and foremost, our world revolves around ourselves. Instead of broadening our horizon, we concentrate on **(Q7)** ... **(reflect)**, meditation and self-development. Searching for our inner god or goddess has become the ultimate goal in terms of personal development. While this is not necessarily negative, the focus we put on ourselves might lead to a lack of **(Q8)** ... **(consider)** and compassion for the people around us. While it might be important to be concerned with ourselves every now and then, we should never **(Q9)** ... **(estimate)** the value of love and friendship as well as the joy it brings to support others in fulfilling their dreams.

0	*majority*	**Q5**	_____
Q1	_____	**Q6**	_____
Q2	_____	**Q7**	_____
Q3	_____	**Q8**	_____
Q4	_____	**Q9**	_____

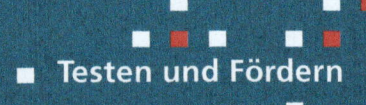
6. Language in use: Is there still an American Dream?

You are going to read a text about the American Dream. Some words are missing from the text. Choose the correct answer (A, B, C or D) for each gap (1–10) in the text. Write your answers in the boxes provided. The first one (0) has been done for you.

Is there still an American Dream?

The American Dream represents the ideal life most Americans desire, including an amazing job with a high **(0)** ..., a perfect little family and a nice home. Only a few decades ago thousands of families in America lived an almost perfect life in **(Q1)** ... and with seemingly endless great opportunities. Unfortunately, the times when it was rather easy to go from rags to **(Q2)** ... seem to be over. In times of economic **(Q3)** ... it has become much harder to hold on to a job or save up a little money, let alone acquire enough wealth to make bigger **(Q4)** ..., such as property. Many people are even **(Q5)** ... to afford health insurance for their family or to fix broken **(Q6)** ... around the house.

In addition, many private households have **(Q7)** ... high amounts of debt, which in turn makes it impossible for them to pay their everyday bills in the long run. This situation has been caused by the development of a society made up of consumers who are used to having everything at their beck and call at any time a day. **(Q8)** ... out credits and loans can therefore be seen as a result of the desire to **(Q9)** ... a high standard of living, even though the **(Q10)** ... circumstances have changed entirely. In contrast to the abundant wealth the American society was used to they will have to move on to a time of saving and dreaming on a smaller scale.

ōbv © Österreichischer Bundesverlag Schulbuch GmbH & Co. KG, Wien 2014 | Alle Rechte vorbehalten | www.oebv.at | www.testen-und-foerdern.at
Prime Time 8. Testen und Fördern, Arbeitsheft (ISBN 978-3-209-08444-6)

0	A income	B payment	C profits	D returns
Q1	A riches	B prosperity	C affluence	D opulence
Q2	A richer	B riches	C rich	D richest
Q3	A collapse	B boom	C recession	D prosperity
Q4	A purchases	B purchasing	C gains	D gaining
Q5	A struggling	B managing	C succeeding	D harassing
Q6	A applications	B designs	C appliances	D goods
Q7	A gathered	B increased	C hoarded	D accumulated
Q8	A taking	B getting	C borrowing	D lending
Q9	A retain	B maintain	C sustain	D contain
Q10	A ergonomical	B ecological	C economical	D economic

0	Q1	Q2	Q3	Q4	Q5	Q6	Q7	Q8	Q9	Q10
A										

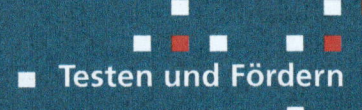
7. Writing: How beautiful do you have to appear on TV? (Article)

The topic of beauty has always been a controversial one. After a discussion in class about the extreme beauty requirements for actors and actresses appearing on TV or in films, you decide to write an **article** on this topic for the school newspaper. In your article, you should:

- explain the importance of beauty in today's society and in the media
- outline the requirements on famous peoples' appearance and discuss whether they are realistic
- refer to the dangers such images might present to teenagers and children

Write an **article** of about **250 words**.

öbv © Österreichischer Bundesverlag Schulbuch GmbH & Co. KG, Wien 2014 | Alle Rechte vorbehalten | www.oebv.at | www.testen-und-foerdern.at
Prime Time 8. Testen und Fördern, Arbeitsheft (ISBN 978-3-209-08444-6)

Fertigkeit	Task	Format	Themenbereich	GERS	Skills
Listening	The conflict of individualism	MC	• Einstellungen und Werte • Umwelt und Gesellschaft	Kann im direkten Kontakt und in den Medien gesprochene Standardsprache verstehen, wenn es um vertraute oder auch um weniger vertraute Themen geht, wie man ihnen normalerweise im privaten, gesellschaftlichen, beruflichen Leben oder in der Ausbildung begegnet. Nur extreme Hintergrundgeräusche, unangemessene Diskursstrukturen oder starke Idiomatik beeinträchtigen das Verständnis.	Listening for specific information/important details; Listening for main ideas and supporting details
Listening	Does globalis-ation threaten our national identity?	NF	• Gedanken, Empfindungen und Gefühle • Umwelt und Gesellschaft	Kann die Hauptaussagen von inhaltlich und sprachlich komplexen Redebeiträgen zu konkreten und abstrakten Themen verstehen, wenn Standardsprache gesprochen wird; versteht auch Fachdiskussionen im eigenen Spezialgebiet. Kann längeren Redebeiträgen und komplexer Argumen-tation folgen, sofern die Thematik einigermaßen vertraut ist und der Rede- oder Gesprächsverlauf durch explizite Signale gekennzeichnet ist.	Listening for specific information/important details; Listening for main ideas and supporting details
Reading	The misery of illegal aliens	MC	• Umwelt und Gesellschaft • Einstellungen und Werte	Kann sehr selbstständig lesen, Lesestil und -tempo verschiedenen Texten und Zwecken anpassen und geeignete Nachschlagewerke selektiv benutzen. Verfügt über einen großen Lesewortschatz, hat aber möglicherweise Schwierigkeiten mit seltener gebrauchten Wendungen.	Reading for specific information; Reading for important details; Reading for main ideas and support details

MC = Multiple choice | NF = Note form | NFQ = Note form with questions | WF = Word formation

Testen und Fördern

Fertigkeit	Task	Format	Themenbereich	GERS	Skills
Reading	Peace – Mission Impossible?	NFQ	• Umwelt und Gesellschaft • Einstellungen und Werte	Kann sehr selbstständig lesen, Lesestil und -tempo verschiedenen Texten und Zwecken anpassen und geeignete Nachschlagewerke selektiv benutzen. Verfügt über einen großen Lesewortschatz, hat aber möglicherweise Schwierigkeiten mit seltener gebrauchten Wendungen.	Reading for specific information; Reading for important details; Reading for main ideas and support details
LiU	Do our own needs surpass our compassion for others?	WF	• Einstellungen und Werte • Umwelt und Gesellschaft		
LiU	Is there still an American Dream?	MC	• Umwelt und Gesellschaft • Interkulturelle und landeskundliche Aspekte		
Writing	TV and beauty	Article	• Einstellungen und Werte • Umwelt und Gesellschaft • Kultur, Medien und Literatur	Kann klare, detaillierte Texte zu verschiedenen Themen aus ihrem/seinem Interessengebiet verfassen und dabei Informationen und Argumente aus verschiedenen Quellen zusammenführen und gegeneinander abwägen.	

MC = Multiple choice | NF = Note form | NFQ = Note form with questions | WF = Word formation

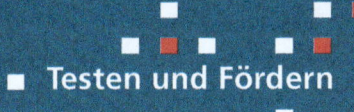
Fertigkeit	Task	Format	Entsprechung in Schülerbuch Prime Time 8
Listening	The conflict of individualism	MC	• A final peace? (p. 9, ex. 1) – MC • Severn Suzuki's speech at the Summit (p. 24, ex. 2) – MC • Home is where the heart is (p. 53, ex. 1) – MC • A taboo topic (p. 84, ex. 2) – MC • I just want to do business (p. 108, ex. 3) – MC • Male and female usage of new technologies (p. 134, ex. 3) – MC
Listening	Does globalisation threaten our national identity?	NF	• Address at the Royal Institute of International Affairs (p. 56, ex. 2) – NF • Outlet shopping (p. 88, ex. 1) – NF • Politically correct Christmas (p. 113, ex. 2) – NF • Reflections of a former British Muslim extremist (p. 133, ex. 1) – NF
Reading	The misery of illegal aliens	MC	• Television (p. 32, ex. 1) – MC • NGOs at work in China (p. 64, ex. 2) – MC • How stem cells can turn back the biological clock (p. 94, ex. 2) – MC • Text speak in well-reputed dictionaries (p. 129, ex. 3) – MC

MC = Multiple choice | NF = Note form | NFQ = Note form with questions | WF = Word formation

Fertigkeit	Task	Format	Entsprechung in Schülerbuch Prime Time 8
Reading	Peace – Mission Impossible?	NFQ	• Barbie goes green (p. 22, ex. 1) – NF • Attentive acupuncturist (p. 44, ex. 2) – NF • Network for Good (p. 68, ex. 2) – NF • "Gap year" before college gives graduates valuable life experience (p. 118, ex. 2) – NF • Don't reduce student loans (p. 124, ex. 2) – NF • Undernutrition in teenage years can lead to heart disease (p. 127, ex. 1) – NF
LiU	Do our own needs surpass our compassion for others?	WF	• The future of Green America (p. 27, ex. 3) – WF • Canada: New pioneers (p. 52, ex. 2) – WF • Word formation (p. 86, ex. 2) – WF • Combatting climate change (p. 138, ex. 3) – WF
LiU	Is there still an American Dream?	MC	• Green shopping? (p. 26, ex. 1) – MC • Formal English (p. 62, ex. 1) – MC • Safe online shopping (p. 89, ex. 3) – MC • Stem cells (p. 101, ex. 4) – MC • Why Facebook searches on job hunters should be banned (p. 138, ex. 4) – MC

MC = Multiple choice | NF = Note form | NFQ = Note form with questions | WF = Word formation

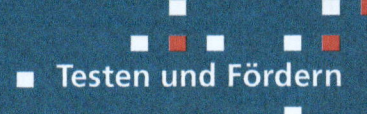

1. Listening: The secret of writing a book

🔊 **You are going to listen to a lecture on the secret behind writing successful books. First you will have 45 seconds to study the task below, then you will hear the recording twice. While listening, complete the sentences (1–5) using a maximum of four words. Write your answers in the spaces provided. The first one (0) has been done for you. After the second listening you will have 45 seconds to check your answers.**

The secret of writing a book

0	Matthew Hamilton promises the participants of his seminar to become	*successful authors*
Q1	According to Hamilton, he differs from other authors because he	
Q2	Creating a storyline for a book is fascinating, because you are free to	
Q3	The technique the author uses to create characters allows him to	
Q4	New authors have to choose their own ... to writing a book.	
Q5	Hamilton admits to having	

✳ ōbv © Österreichischer Bundesverlag Schulbuch GmbH & Co. KG, Wien 2014 | Alle Rechte vorbehalten | www.oebv.at | www.testen-und-foerdern.at
Prime Time 8. Testen und Fördern, Arbeitsheft (ISBN 978-3-209-08444-6)

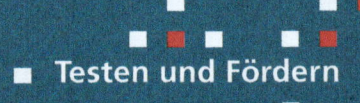
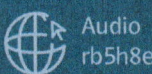
2. Listening: The biggest lies about beauty

You are going to listen to a recording about the biggest lies about beauty. First you will have 45 seconds to study the task below, then you will hear the recording twice. While listening, match the beginnings of the sentences (1–5) with the sentence endings (A–H). There are two extra sentence endings you should not use. Write your answers in the spaces provided. The first one (0) has been done for you. After the second listening you will have 45 seconds to check your answers.

The biggest lies about beauty

0	The radio host starts out by …	E
Q1	People around the world and their ideas on beauty are …	
Q2	Young adults' images of beauty are …	
Q3	The conflict between realistic views and society's requirements results in people …	
Q4	In their everyday lives, people can't avoid …	
Q5	For most patients, cosmetic surgery results in …	

A	… becoming more aware of the situation.
B	… adapting to recent changes.
C	… becoming increasingly different.
D	… being even unhappier.
E	… giving an overview of today's topics.
F	… being developed.
G	… being insecure and disoriented.
H	… being adapted.

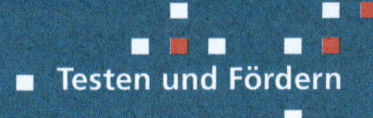

3. Reading: Marriage between homosexual partners

Read the text below, then put the summarising statements (A–I) into the correct order. There are two extra summarising statements you should not use. Write your answers in the boxes provided. The first one (0) has been done for you.

Marriage between homosexual partners

Looking at the changes societal structures went through in recent years, it is not surprising that many people have a hard time adapting to new concepts and laws. While the fact that homosexual relationships exist and are acceptable seems to have sunk in, the idea of legalising marriages between same sex partners is far more critical in the eyes of its opponents.

One argument that is frequently coming up in discussion is the religious aspect of marriage. Since many religions do not accept homosexual relationships, they refuse to celebrate the bond between same sex partners in church and provide them with the possibility to speak their vows in a religious context. However, most homosexual couples do not strive for the church's tolerance but for legal appreciation of their decision to share their life.

When it comes to legal confirmation, opponents of legalising such marriages often claim that the protection and security such a legal bond offers should be reserved for heterosexual couples, who fulfil their image of proper couples. They argue that couples who are likely to raise families are in greater need of such protective laws and regulations than two adults who will never reproduce in a natural way.

Nevertheless, the question remains whether it would not violate basic human rights to refuse couples who fell in love the right to be partners also in a legal sense. This is especially true in reference to possible emergency situations, where homosexual partners often run into problems obtaining even the most basic information about each other from doctors or nurses when their partner has been hospitalised. In addition, people living together should also be able to inherit from each other or to perform other legal action possible for married couples.

However, opponents are often angered by the fact that such a legalisation might provide homosexual couples with financial benefits designed for couples willing to raise a family. In many countries married couples enjoy special forms of tax relief, which would then also be extended to same sex marriages. Nevertheless, this problem could easily be solved by introducing different tax regulations for any childless married couple, no matter whether it is homosexual or heterosexual.

The biggest concern, however, lies in the fact that childless married couples legally have the right to adopt children. If homosexual marriages were legalised, many opponents fear the partners would be eligible to apply for adoption. On the one hand, it is argued that

ōbv © Österreichischer Bundesverlag Schulbuch GmbH & Co. KG, Wien 2014 | Alle Rechte vorbehalten | www.oebv.at | www.testen-und-foerdern.at
Prime Time 8. Testen und Fördern, Arbeitsheft (ISBN 978-3-209-08444-6)

heterosexual couples who cannot naturally conceive should take priority over homosexual couples who made the decision to be with a partner they cannot naturally reproduce with. On the other hand, there is a conflict going on about whether children should be raised in a homosexual environment at all. Many of those presumptions, however, are driven by fear. There is no proof available that this way of raising children has any kind of negative effect on them. In the same spirit we could argue that any person with a habit that is not deemed acceptable or positive should not be allowed to reproduce. Nevertheless, these fears and prejudices towards homosexual couples are difficult to fight and are often rooted deep within the minds of people.

In order to increase tolerance and acceptance, it will be necessary to discuss this topic openly and honestly. By offering both opponents and supporters a platform to voice their concerns, we have the chance to make them understand and accept different points of view and we might actually reach our goal of treating people equally.

A	Homosexual couples are in a different situation, because they will not have any children.
B	Nowadays most people tend to tolerate homosexual relationships.
C	Not all legal actions possible for married couples should be open to same sex partners.
D	Homosexual couples aim for legal acceptance of their relationships.
E	The government would have to change the income laws for childless couples.
F	New laws would make the situation easier on hospital staff.
G	There are many prejudices against homosexual couples raising children.
H	Homosexual partners can't get married in any church.
I	Listening to different opinions about the issue could improve the situation.

0	Q1	Q2	Q3	Q4	Q5	Q6
B						

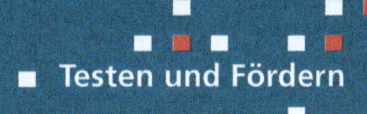
4. Reading: The trouble with internships

Read the text below, then choose the correct heading (A–H) for each paragraph (1–5). There are two extra headings you should not use. Write your answers in the boxes provided at the end of the task. The first one (0) has been done for you.

The trouble with internships

… (0)

Lately most companies place more and more emphasis on work experience when hiring new staff. This, however, presents young people who have just finished their education with a huge problem, since even the best universities cannot provide them with the required practical knowledge. On realising that their chances to find employment are extremely slim without any experience, many people at the beginning of their career decide to enter an internship in order to gain knowledge on the job.

… (Q1)

Most companies do not mind hiring interns, because they provide an easy solution to the problem of covering peak times in production or service. Since especially larger companies have a need of interns, most of them offer similar types of internships. They are usually either not paid at all or present the workers with rather low wages. Additionally, such employment agreements are limited to a certain amount of time from the start and can also be terminated immediately from both parties. Most of these workers will work in assistance positions, since there is little time to train them for a job with higher responsibility. Although their duties resemble those of normal workers, their status does not require them to work independently.

… (Q2)

Before entering an internship, there are certain factors both parties, the employing company as well as the intern, have to clarify. Since firms may have varying work shifts and many interns are still finishing their education or have another job at the same time, both sides have to agree on possible work times. The workload may in many cases be less than that of a normal worker, although this has to be discussed in each individual case. In addition, many employers require proof of education or an impeccable reputation of the applicant

ōbv © Österreichischer Bundesverlag Schulbuch GmbH & Co. KG, Wien 2014 | Alle Rechte vorbehalten | www.oebv.at | www.testen-und-foerdern.at
Prime Time 8. Testen und Fördern, Arbeitsheft (ISBN 978-3-209-08444-6)

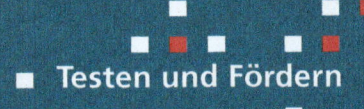
before hiring the intern. Only after making sure the requirements are met, a contract will be formed. Finally, signing non-disclosure clauses might be necessary in order to protect the company's product.

... (Q3)

Clearly internships have many possible benefits for young people. However, it is not always the case that such employment guarantees a job offer later on. Naturally many interns hope to be kept on by the company after a few months, but fail to realise that companies often have underlying reasons for employing interns that have nothing to do with later hiring. In addition, internships do not ensure that the worker gains experience in the area they are interested in or were aiming at. Finally, there is the question of income. The lack of payment for the work can cause major difficulties for interns.

... (Q4)

In the ideal case internships would simply be the perfect opportunity to first enter the job market. Once you have signed a contract for a position like that, it opens the door to making your first steps in a small or large company. Not always, however, does this decision prove to be a good one. As a matter of fact, interns work in relatively low positions, which often invite condescending behaviour of their superiors or even sexual harassment. Even if such incidents cannot be seen as normal occurrences, a raised awareness towards them might be necessary. Furthermore, the possibility of being used as a cheap worker instead of being instructed on appropriate work duties is a very real one.

... (Q5)

On the other hand, the assignments given to interns may be quite complex and challenging. Given that many people with internship contracts have received an excellent education, they are usually thought to be capable of performing certain high-skill duties, provided that they do not need any extra training on them. Same as normal workers, interns should do their jobs in the best way possible and be aware of the fact that they represent the company at any time. Being aware of this fact will help in succeeding during your internship.

ōbv © Österreichischer Bundesverlag Schulbuch GmbH & Co. KG, Wien 2014 | Alle Rechte vorbehalten | www.oebv.at | www.testen-und-foerdern.at
Prime Time 8. Testen und Fördern, Arbeitsheft (ISBN 978-3-209-08444-6)

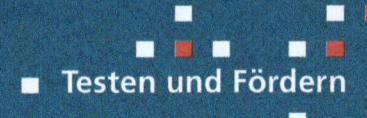

A	Drawbacks of internships
B	The new-found importance of internships
C	Laws for internships
D	Risks of entering such types of employment
E	Common similarities of internships
F	Possible consequences of internships
G	Expectations on interns
H	Agreements between interns and companies

0	Q1	Q2	Q3	Q4	Q5
B					

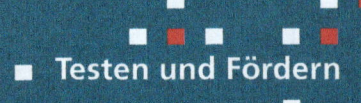
5. Language in use: The significance of being different

You are going to read a text about the significance of being different. In most lines of the text there is a word that should not be there. Write that word in the space provided after each line. Seven to nine lines are correct. Indicate these lines with a tick (✓). There are two examples at the beginning.

The significance of being different

Younger generations have always aimed at being **as** different from the	as	0
generations before them, mostly because they commonly feel the need to	✓	00
establish their own style, identity, and way of life. The result is a huge gap		Q1
between older and younger members of society, which in the turn causes		Q2
major conflicts and frequent disagreements.		Q3
Another consequence out of this fact is the perception of younger people		Q4
as to being disrespectful and ungrateful towards their elders, even though		Q5
most young adults' efforts to be different rather originate in their desire to		Q6
create something new than in their wish to overthrow what others will		Q7
have worked for or to rebel against anything and anybody.		Q8
However, among of members of one generation the basic ideals and		Q9
expectations on life are normally quite so similar. Up until now most		Q10
people belonging to a specific age of group tended to display certain		Q11
types of hairstyle, clothes, and behaviour. Nevertheless, the members of		Q12
recent generations show a tendency towards the placing an increased		Q13
importance on being individuals who differ from each and other. This rise		Q14
in individualism is especially noticeable when it comes to the way people		Q15
behave in society, which is becoming increasingly extrovert and outspoken.		Q16

✳ ōbv © Österreichischer Bundesverlag Schulbuch GmbH & Co. KG, Wien 2014 | Alle Rechte vorbehalten | www.oebv.at | www.testen-und-foerdern.at
Prime Time 8. Testen und Fördern, Arbeitsheft (ISBN 978-3-209-08444-6)

6. Language in use: Successful businessmen and -women

You are going to read a text about businesspeople. Some words are missing from the text. Fill in the word which best fits each gap (1–7). Use only one word in each gap. Write your answers in the spaces provided at the end of the text. The first one (0) has been done for you.

Successful businessmen and -women

Most successful businessmen and -women are well aware **(0)** ... the envy they are constantly met with. It is no secret that most of us see wealth, power and influence as something to aspire to. Nevertheless, most people on top of the food **(Q1)** ... did not simply reap the benefits of their parents' lifelong work, but put endless hours into **(Q2)** ... their set goals. They know that it is hard work to stay where they are at and that one tiny mistake can be the cause of their downfall.

In **(Q3)** ... to become a successful manager, there are certain character traits you should possess. To begin with, you have to be dedicated to your profession and willing to learn every little aspect of it. The more you know about the individual aspects of your company or department, **(Q4)** ... more likely it is that you make informed and useful decisions. In addition, knowledge about marketing **(Q5)** ..., economic principles, and accounting is necessary to ensure you are doing a good job as a manager.

Naturally, there are many benefits to pursuing a successful career. Once you have made it, there are rewards far **(Q6)** ... what most other people receive for doing their jobs. Nevertheless, the risks you take are equally extreme, since businessmen and -women rank among the groups with the highest risk of burn out or depression and suffering **(Q7)** ... physical symptoms of stress, such as ulcers.

0	of
Q1	
Q2	
Q3	
Q4	
Q5	
Q6	
Q7	

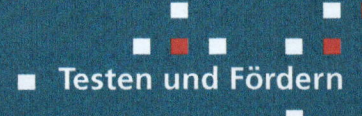
7. Writing: Money matters (Formal letter)

As a student you have noticed a clear increase in excursions and projects. While you understand their purpose, you also see the high costs of such activities. As a head student, you write a **formal letter** to the headmaster, Mr Sawyer, to make him aware of the problem. In your formal letter, you should:

- outline the problem you see in the increased costs for students
- describe the financial consequences on low-income families and their children
- recommend an alternative solution for this problem

Write a **formal letter** of about **250 words**.

✳ ōbv © Österreichischer Bundesverlag Schulbuch GmbH & Co. KG, Wien 2014 | Alle Rechte vorbehalten | www.oebv.at | www.testen-und-foerdern.at
Prime Time 8. Testen und Fördern, Arbeitsheft (ISBN 978-3-209-08444-6)

Fertigkeit	Task	Format	Themenbereich	GERS	Skills
Listening	The secret behind writing books	NF	• Umwelt und Gesellschaft • Schule und Arbeitswelt • Kultur, Medien und Literatur	Kann im direkten Kontakt und in den Medien gesprochene Standardsprache verstehen, wenn es um vertraute oder auch um weniger vertraute Themen geht, wie man ihnen normalerweise im privaten, gesellschaftlichen, beruflichen Leben oder in der Ausbildung begegnet. Nur extreme Hintergrundgeräusche, unangemessene Diskursstrukturen oder starke Idiomatik beeinträchtigen das Verständnis.	Listening for specific information/important details; Listening for main ideas and supporting details
Listening	The biggest lies about beauty	MM	• Einstellungen und Werte • Umwelt und Gesellschaft	Kann im direkten Kontakt und in den Medien gesprochene Standardsprache verstehen, wenn es um vertraute oder auch um weniger vertraute Themen geht, wie man ihnen normalerweise im privaten, gesellschaftlichen, beruflichen Leben oder in der Ausbildung begegnet. Nur extreme Hintergrundgeräusche, unangemessene Diskursstrukturen oder starke Idiomatik beeinträchtigen das Verständnis.	Listening for specific information/important details; Listening for main ideas and supporting details
Reading	Marriage between homo-sexual partners	S	• Umwelt und Gesellschaft • Einstellungen und Werte	Kann sehr selbstständig lesen, Lesestil und -tempo verschiedenen Texten und Zwecken anpassen und geeignete Nachschlagewerke selektiv benutzen. Verfügt über einen großen Lesewortschatz, hat aber möglicherweise Schwierigkeiten mit seltener gebrauchten Wendungen.	Reading for specific information; Reading for important details; Reading for main ideas and support details

ED = Editing | MM = Multiple matching | NF = Note form | OGF = Open gap fill | S= Sequencing

ōbv © Österreichischer Bundesverlag Schulbuch GmbH & Co. KG, Wien 2014 | Alle Rechte vorbehalten | www.oebv.at | www.testen-und-foerdern.at
Prime Time 8. Testen und Fördern, Arbeitsheft (ISBN 978-3-209-08444-6)

Fertigkeit	Task	Format	Themenbereich	GERS	Skills
Reading	The trouble with internships	MM	• Umwelt und Gesellschaft • Einstellungen und Werte • Schule und Arbeitswelt	Kann sehr selbstständig lesen, Lesestil und -tempo verschiedenen Texten und Zwecken anpassen und geeignete Nachschlagewerke selektiv benutzen. Verfügt über einen großen Lesewortschatz, hat aber möglicherweise Schwierigkeiten mit seltener gebrauchten Wendungen.	Reading for specific information; Reading for important details; Reading for main ideas and support details
LiU	The significance of being different	ED	• Einstellungen und Werte • Umwelt und Gesellschaft		
LiU	Successful business-men and -women	OGF	• Umwelt und Gesellschaft • Schule und Arbeitswelt • Gedanken, Empfindungen und Gefühle		
Writing	Money matters	Formal letter	• Einstellungen und Werte • Umwelt und Gesellschaft • Schule und Arbeitswelt	Kann klare, detaillierte Texte zu verschiedenen Themen aus ihrem/seinem Interessengebiet verfassen und dabei Informationen und Argumente aus verschiedenen Quellen zusammenführen und gegeneinander abwägen.	

ED = Editing | MM = Multiple matching | NF = Note form | OGF = Open gap fill | S= Sequencing

ōbv © Österreichischer Bundesverlag Schulbuch GmbH & Co. KG, Wien 2014 | Alle Rechte vorbehalten | www.oebv.at | www.testen-und-foerdern.at
Prime Time 8. Testen und Fördern, Arbeitsheft (ISBN 978-3-209-08444-6)

Fertigkeit	Task	Format	Entsprechung in Schülerbuch Prime Time 8
Listening	The secret behind writing books	NF	• Address at the Royal Institute of International Affairs (p. 56, ex. 2) – NF • Outlet shopping (p. 88, ex. 1) – NF • Politically correct Christmas (p. 113, ex. 2) – NF • Reflections of a former British Muslim extremist (p. 133, ex. 1) – NF
Listening	The biggest lies about beauty	MM	• An Inconvenient Truth (p. 28, ex. 2) – MM • Interview – Part 2 (p. 48, ex. 4) – MM • Choosing my religion – It's normal in the US (p. 73, ex. 3) – MM • The language of science (p. 99, ex. 1) – MM • What to think of gap years (p. 119, ex. 3) – MM • Panel discussion about climate change (p. 134, ex. 2) – MM
Reading	Marriage between homosexual partners	S	• Single and happy – It's the freemales (p. 70, ex. 2) – S • Could vegetarians eat a "test tube" burger? (p. 132, ex. 5) – S

ED = Editing | MM = Multiple matching | OGF = Open gap fill | NF = Note form | S= Sequencing

✳ ōbv © Österreichischer Bundesverlag Schulbuch GmbH & Co. KG, Wien 2014 | Alle Rechte vorbehalten | www.oebv.at | www.testen-und-foerdern.at
Prime Time 8. Testen und Fördern, Arbeitsheft (ISBN 978-3-209-08444-6)

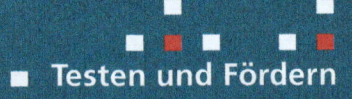
Fertigkeit	Task	Format	Entsprechung in Schülerbuch Prime Time 8
Reading	The trouble with internships	MM	• Coming back home (p. 16, ex. 1) – MM • Two opposing views (p. 50, ex. 1) – MM • Impressions from the Seeds of Peace summer camp (p. 58, ex. 2) – MM • Hero – Tariq Jahan (p. 75, ex. 1) – MM • Slavery (p. 112, ex. 1) – MM • Stop the press! The future of US journalism (p. 128, ex. 2) – MM
LiU	The significance of being different	ED	• Mars (p. 17, ex. 3) – ED • Editing (p. 65, ex. 3) – ED • Brightworks (p. 125, ex. 4) – ED • Increase of obesity (p. 139, ex. 5) – ED
LiU	Successful businessmen and -women	OGF	• Transsexuality (p. 41, ex. 3) – OGF • Youth "cannot live" without web (p. 137, ex. 2) – OGF

ED = Editing | MM = Multiple matching | OGF = Open gap fill | NF = Note form | S= Sequencing

1. Listening: Will boys still be boys?

You are going to listen to an interview about child development. First you will have 45 seconds to study the task below, then you will hear the recording twice. While listening, choose the correct answer (A, B, C or D) for questions 1–5. Put a ☒ in the correct box. The first one (0) has been done for you. After the second listening you will have 45 seconds to check your answers.

Will boys still be boys?

0 How often does "Modern Psychology" go on air?

- A once a day ☐
- B once a week ☒
- C once in two weeks ☐
- D once a month ☐

Q1 What was Dr Umbridge's main motivation to choose this line of work?

- A She was fascinated by the human mind. ☐
- B She wanted to understand the functions of the human mind. ☐
- C She wanted to help children express their anxieties. ☐
- D She wanted to change children's life for the better. ☐

Q2 Dr Umbridge's book points out that

- A boys cause more troubles growing up than girls. ☐
- B parents expect more from boys than ever before. ☐
- C mental disorders can be caused by negative experiences. ☐
- D boys have problems in dealing with their current environment. ☐

Q3 What does Dr Umbridge see as the main cause for the boys' problems?

- A There has been an increase in the number of divorces. ☐
- B Boys are confused about society's expectations. ☐
- C There has been a change in societal and family conditions. ☐
- D Boys feel put under pressure by their parents. ☐

Q4 According to Dr Umbridge, what tends to cause boys to develop OCDs?

- A Their fathers force them to suppress their feelings. ☐
- B One of their parents displays aggressive behavior. ☐
- C They grow up in a family with very strict rules. ☐
- D They do not know how to react to their parents' expectations. ☐

Q5 Why do boys struggle more with modern family structures than girls?

- A They have to figure out their new place in society. ☐
- B They need to accept a new set of values. ☐
- C They prefer the traditional hierarchical family structures. ☐
- D They are presented with higher expectations. ☐

▼4

▼5

ōbv © Österreichischer Bundesverlag Schulbuch GmbH & Co. KG, Wien 2014 | Alle Rechte vorbehalten | www.oebv.at | www.testen-und-foerdern.at
Prime Time 8. Testen und Fördern, Arbeitsheft (ISBN 978-3-209-08444-6)

KEY

- 0—B   once a week
- Q1—D   She wanted to change children's life for the better.
- Q2—D   Boys have problems in dealing with their current environment.
- Q3—B   Boys are confused about society's expectations.
- Q4—C   They grow up in a family with very strict rules.
- Q5—A   They have to figure out their new place in society.

TAPESCRIPT

Male host	Good morning and welcome to "Modern Psychology", your favourite Monday night radio magazine. This is Tyron McBell, welcoming Dr Sasha Umbridge, today's guest on the show. She has been considered the leading expert in matters of child psychology for over 15 years and is willing to share her knowledge about the increased hardships boys suffer when growing up in modern society. It is great to have you here today, Dr Umbridge.
Dr Umbridge	Thank you very much, Mr McBell. I am excited to be a guest on your show.
Male host	Before we dive into the topic at hand, would you mind elaborating a little on your reasons for choosing this specific profession?
Dr Umbridge	Well, apart from the fact that I have always been fascinated with the human mind and the way it functions, I felt that this was an opportunity to make a real difference in people's lives, more specifically in children's lives. In most cases they have a much harder time expressing their fears and anxieties and often refrain from asking for help when they need it.
Male host	Over the last few years you main area of research focused on the troubles especially boys face when growing up. In your latest book, you claim that the current upsurge in mental disorders and difficulties many boys experience result more from them than ever before. So what exactly are those changes you are referring to?
Dr Umbridge	Uhm, as you can imagine, the newly evolving societal structures, caused by developments, such as single parenting, patchwork families and higher divorce rates, are part of the problem. Of course, these affect female children as well as male ones. However, we have noticed an increase in pressure on young boys in particular, when it comes to the way they are raised and expected to develop. The biggest challenge lies in the range of character traits and behaviour they should be able to display, since they will be confused about what exactly they are asked to do and be.
Male host	So basically we are moving away from clear-cut stereotypical gender roles?
Dr Umbridge	That is exactly what is causing the difficulties mentioned. Not only are boys supposed to display all kinds of traditional values, such as courage, bravery, or strength, but they are expected to be in contact with their softer, more feminine side at the same time. To put it bluntly, their fathers still raise them to be strong family providers who strive to suppress their feelings while their mothers teach them to be sensitive and capable of talking about their deepest emotions. Many boys simply do not know where to turn to and rebel by displaying more aggressive behaviour towards one of the parents. Other consequences, commonly found in a more oppressive family environment, are a lack of self-confidence and a tendency towards obsessive compulsive disorders, or OCDs.
Male host	It seems that teaching boys to be more emotional would turn out to be beneficial. For a while now experts have been pointing out why old-fashioned patterns from former times tend to be problematic. So why do our future men run into such problems?
Dr Umbridge	There is no doubt that society needs to adapt to current changes and that many changes have been more than overdue. However, the problems result from different expectations towards the two sexes. While girls enjoy having more choices and becoming more equal to men, their male counterparts seem a little lost. They have not yet found their new role in this world. Thus, they struggle to make sense of what is going on and how they fit into the modern family, where hierarchical structures have no place any more. This means parents need to adapt, communicate with each other and teach their sons an entirely new set of values.
Male host	Well, does that mean that parents must be held responsible for the recently occurring psychological problems of male children and teenage boys?
Dr Umbridge	Certainly not! The point I am trying to make is that, seeing what is happening, we need to equip future parents with advice on how to go new ways in raising their children. Uhm, I would even go as far as to say that a high percentage of parents seem to be doing an awesome job raising their sons to be future fathers and husbands, considering that today's parents were brought up entirely differently themselves.
Male host	Well, thank you so much, Dr Umbridge, for answering all of my questions. Now we would like to give our listeners a chance to pick your brain. Here is our first caller ... (fade out)

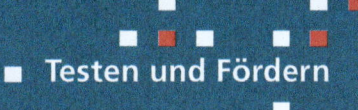
KEY

0–E	participate in an interview about Irish culture.
Q1–B	express their pride in their culture.
Q2–D	follow their families' traditions.
Q3–F	focus on a variety of forms.
Q4–C	listen to Irish musicians.
Q5–G	inquire more about their own culture.

▼6

2. Listening: Are young Irish still traditional?

You are going to listen to a recording about whether young Irish people are still interested in culture. First you will have 45 seconds to study the task below, then you will hear the recording twice. While listening, match the beginnings of the sentences (1–5) with the sentence endings (A–H). There are two extra sentence endings you should not use. Write your answers in the spaces provided. The first one (0) has been done for you. After the second listening you will have 45 seconds to check your answers.

Are young Irish still traditional?

0	Roberta and Steven have agreed to …	E
Q1	The majority of the Irish are happy to …	
Q2	Teenagers in Ireland tend to …	
Q3	Irish humour is known to …	
Q4	Steven thinks that occasionally it is OK to …	
Q5	Irish teenagers have started to …	

A	… play a typical Irish instrument.
B	… express their pride in their culture.
C	… listen to Irish musicians.
D	… follow their families' traditions.
E	… participate in an interview about Irish culture.
F	… focus on a variety of forms.
G	… inquire more about their own culture.
H	… spread their culture.

▼6

TAPESCRIPT

Interviewer	Welcome, Roberta and Steven, and thank you so much for agreeing to take part in an interview for our magazine, "Cultures of Europe". Since both of you are young adults residing in Ireland, more precisely in Kinsale, a small but charming town in County Cork, I hope you will be able to describe the significance Irish culture still has for teenagers like you. Uhm, I believe, you are both 17, so would you say that there are cultural aspects that are more interesting for young adults than for older age groups?
Roberta Green	Well, in general it must be said that the Irish culture is a very rich one. Many Irish are proud of their roots and heritage and they are not reluctant to express this opinion. I know hardly anyone who is not involved in an activity connected to art, literature or music. It does not matter if they belong to younger or older generations, there is simply this amazing focus on doing something that goes beyond living your daily life. However, I believe that most people my age are strongly influenced by their familial environment and … and by how their closest relatives deal with culture and tradition. So I would say that it depends on what teenagers have experienced what cultural aspects they put most emphasis on.
Interviewer	I believe you have a point there, Roberta. Now Steven, what aspect of Irish culture are you most fascinated by?
Steven Jones	Uhm, hm, it's really difficult to choose just one, because there are so many areas I am interested in. Of course there is literature, especially since our country has always been home to so many great authors. Just think of Wilde or Yeats and their works. But if I had to, I would probably go with Irish humour. The Irish have a long history of telling amusing stories, creating clever limericks and making up new jokes. Just the other day, I heard a hilarious one about a witch and a leprechaun. I wish I could think of it now … well, anyways, over the past few years, a strong comedy scene has been emerging, which celebrates Irish humour in a whole different way and also makes it easier for our culture to be appreciated all over the world.
Interviewer	I agree, I have always loved the Irish humour. I hope you will remember this joke of yours by the end of the interview.
Steven Jones	We'll see …
Interviewer	Whenever I went to Ireland, I never missed the chance to enjoy the atmosphere in a pub and listen to some Irish music. How do you feel about this part of Irish culture, Steven?
Steven Jones	I have to admit, there are also other music styles that I enjoy listening to, but there are times, for example at traditional celebrations, such as weddings or St Patrick's Day, when I don't mind hearing some Irish musicians play their instruments. Well, I guess you really aren't Irish, if you don't like the sound of the harp, are you?
Interviewer	Well, it is a symbol for Ireland after all. What about you, Roberta? Are you into Irish music at all?
Roberta Green	I like it, yes, especially the instruments. I play the fiddle myself, actually. When I grew up, my parents insisted on me taking lessons and I could not avoid learning to play the one or the other traditional tune. I spend less time practising today, but there is a certain magic to Irish music which some other music styles are definitely lacking.
Interviewer	Oh that is definitely true. As a last question, in terms of young adults, do you think that their interest in Ireland's culture is generally decreasing?
Roberta Green	Well, there might be some trends which point in this direction, but actually I see a rise in young people taking up hobbies connected to important cultural areas. Thus, I would probably say that the problem is not a big one in Ireland.
Steven Jones	I'd have to agree with Roberta. Even older relatives of mine have commented on young people asking increasingly many questions. It almost seems as if the younger generation refuses to lose any cultural treasures from the past.
Interviewer	Thank you, Steven and Roberta, for answering my questions so patiently. We will send you a copy of the article!
Steven Jones	Ah, that's grand … you are welcome! And I'll email you the joke, if it ever comes to mind again … what was it …
Roberta Green	It was our pleasure.

3. Reading: Trends in advertising

Read the text below, then complete the sentences (1–6) using a maximum of four words. Write your answers in the spaces provided. The first one (0) has been done for you.

Trends in advertising

Due to the pressure on businesses to increase their sales on the one hand and to reduce their costs on the other hand, the role of advertising in the media has become increasingly significant. While companies in former times relied mainly on televised advertisements, today the internet presents the biggest pool of possible customers.

Advertising has always been blamed for being rather stereotypical, since it usually displays quite unrealistic scenarios and images of perfect families, stunningly beautiful people and impossibly cute pets. The depiction of the real world is commonly not thought to be appealing enough to persuade customers to purchase certain products and to choose them over other rivalling brands.

Naturally, the way the two genders are portrayed in advertising has an enormous influence on how we perceive the products presented. Taking a closer look at the role of women in advertising, for example, it becomes obvious that certain types of women with specific characteristics appear more frequently than others.

Despite the fact that a few decades ago women were mainly cast for the role of a housewife, today advertisements tend to depict young, successful businesswomen, who are self-confident and independent. Younger audiences in particular appreciate the changes made, because they have an easier time to empathise with characters who try to achieve similar goals, such as professional success or personal well-being.

Due to these recent developments producers involved in the advertising business have also made changes to spots aimed at older target groups. These changes place an emphasis on how to enjoy a pleasant life after retirement and concentrate on products commonly not needed or used by younger viewers. Nevertheless, the spots produced do not portray the actors starring as elderly people who are approaching the end of their lives. On the contrary, a growing number of advertisements shows lively, athletic 60- to 70-year-olds who are only starting to realise how much they still want to achieve.

In addition, recent spots on TV are pleasantly lacking the formerly so strongly emphasised perfection. A strong tendency towards imperfection can be detected, which is a very different approach in comparison to former years. It almost seems as if the audience has grown tired of being reminded what they themselves will most likely never have or be. More realistic advertisements provide us with a sense of comfort and satisfaction, because they leave us room to accept our own weaknesses and problems. Since the pressure of the modern world on all of us is steadily rising, it comes as no surprise that few viewers feel the desire to experience perfection in advertising.

However, the rules change when men form the main target group of a certain commercial. While women are perfectly happy to sympathise with imperfect female actors, men do not necessarily enjoy these new developments and expect to find certain stereotypes fulfilled in advertisements aiming at them. Thus, more and more production companies find themselves torn between meeting the expectations of modern women and still somewhat patriarchal men.

0	The most important medium for advertising is … .	*the internet*
Q1	People accuse advertisements of … .	
Q2	Too many references to reality might not lead to … .	
Q3	Recent adjustments in advertising especially appeal to … .	
Q4	The main focus of advertisements for older generations is on … .	
Q5	In former times, imperfection … .	
Q6	The gap in men's and women's ideas on advertising … .	

KEY

0   the internet.
Q1   being stereotypical/displaying unrealistic scenarios/being too unrealistic.
Q2   customers buying advertised products/customers choosing certain products.
Q3   younger audiences/younger people.
Q4   life after retirement/products for older people.
Q5   was avoided/was unwanted in advertising.
Q6   influences production companies/causes problems for producers.

4. Reading: The challenges of going green

Read the text below, then decide whether the statements (1–7) are true (T) or false (F) and put a ☒ in the correct box. Then identify the sentence in the text which supports your decision. Write the first four words of this sentence in the spaces provided. The first one (0) has been done for you.

The challenges of going green

After hundreds of years it seems that the human race has finally grasped that the planet's environment cannot continue to be corrupted any further. Already we suffer from the severe consequences, such as climate change, ozone layer depletion, extreme weather conditions, and destruction of the ocean's flora and fauna. However, this might only have been the start of a chain of events, if no action is taken to end this vicious circle of devastation.

These problems can mostly be traced back to an increase in energy consumption. The demand for all forms of energy, which has exploded over the past decade due to the rise of the world's population as well as its industry, has become almost impossible to meet for even the biggest energy corporations, due to the declining supply of natural resources. As a result, scientific research has focused on the development of alternative forms of energy production. The main problem lies in the fact that there is no consensus of which type of alternative solution should be favoured among scientists.

Among the various choices for clean energy production, three methods are most commonly used: wind, water, and solar energy. While in some cases the regional landscape and weather conditions are the determining factors, at other times economic aspects might influence the decision. Experts often opt for a combination of methods in order to secure energy supply at all times.

Even though several methods have been implemented and are being used successfully around the world, many governments are reluctant to rely on those solutions entirely. Apparently they fear economic drawbacks which might only show once large sums have been invested into these new industries. There is also no guarantee that investments made into alternative energies will produce the expected results. It might well be that seemingly promising methods produce less energy than consumed or prove to be less cost-efficient than thought. Additionally, turning back at this point might not be possible any more, which could result in the dependence of these governments on other states in matters of energy production.

Apart from all those factors, the main challenge lies in making all of the parties involved understand the urgency of responding to the situation. Although the human race will still be able to rely on fossil fuels for some time, they will cease to be available to us at some point. The energy crisis is likely to become more and more of an issue, since resources will not be running out everywhere at the same time. Even in the best of cases scientists, governments, and energy corporations will have to cooperate for years to come up with suitable alternative solutions which can ultimately ensure the growing energy demand will be met. Failure to react now could easily result in a world-wide political and economic crisis.

As of now, there are small steps being taken to improve the current situation. In various countries governments are investing in the research of alternative energy and implement programmes aimed at reducing our negative impact on the environment. The sincerity with which these actions are taken will determine whether they will be successful and whether we can stop ourselves from going down a road that will ultimately lead to our ruin.

	Statement	T	F	Justification
0	Most people have understood that we cannot damage the environment any longer.		X	After hundreds of years
Q1	The problems we experience are very likely to have only been the beginning.			
Q2	Most energy corporations can no longer supply enough energy.			
Q3	Most scientists do not agree on which form of alternative energy is the best one.			
Q4	The location of a country influences its choice of energy production methods.			
Q5	Many countries refuse to use alternative forms of energy entirely.			
Q6	Countries using alternative forms of energy production might overestimate the success of these methods.			
Q7	Actions towards using alternative energy will have to be taken within the next few years to avoid severe consequences.			

▼10

▼9

⁂ ōbv © Österreichischer Bundesverlag Schulbuch GmbH & Co. KG, Wien 2014 | Alle Rechte vorbehalten | www.oebv.at | www.testen-und-foerdern.at
Prime Time 8. Testen und Fördern, Arbeitsheft (ISBN 978-3-209-08444-6)

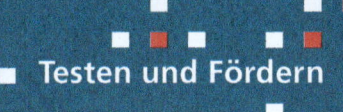

5. Language in use: Voluntary single

You are going to read a text about being single. In most lines of the text there is a word that should not be there. Write that word in the space provided after each line. Nine to eleven lines are correct. Indicate these lines with a tick (✓). There are two examples at the beginning.

Voluntary single

KEY

0	✓
00	out
Q1	of
Q2	✓
Q3	all
Q4	✓
Q5	✓
Q6	✓
Q7	it
Q8	✓
Q9	✓
Q10	only
Q11	✓
Q12	of
Q13	✓
Q14	✓
Q15	✓

While magazines and books present our younger generations with an
endless flood of information on how to find **out** the perfect partner, it
seems that many **of** young adults in their twenties are not even interested
in searching for the one to spend the rest of their lives with. They would
rather focus on their careers, enjoy the world to **all** the fullest, and
experience a phase of selfishness without having yet to consider the
feelings of another human being. After the desperate search conducted
by most generations before them, our youth seems to deal with this topic
in an incredibly relaxed way. So what is it that **it** has changed so much?
For one thing, society has become much more welcoming towards
single people. Entire businesses have focused on the new target
groups of voluntary singles, who have not **only** failed to find a partner, but
lead completely full and happy lives without one. Now that singles have
finally managed to get rid of the stigma of being socially incapable **of**,
especially women often enjoy the benefits being single can have in terms
of their professional careers. However, the question remains whether
these advantages come at too high a cost.

KEY

0–T   After hundreds of years
Q1–T   However, this might only
Q2–F   The demand for all
Q3–T   The main problem lies
Q4–F   While in some cases
Q5–F   Even though several methods
Q6–T   It might well be
Q7–F   Failure to react now

69

▼12

6. Language in use: The responsibilities of superpowers

You are going to read a text about superpowers and their responsibilities towards society. Some words are missing from the text. Use the word in brackets to form a word that fits in the gaps (1–8). Write your answers in the spaces provided at the end of the text. The first one (0) has been done for you.

The responsibilities of superpowers

In our global world people, countries and even continents are **(0)** … **(increase)** interconnected. However, this fact does not only provide us with benefits. Especially for so-called economic superpowers, **(Q1)** … **(global)** comes at a rather high cost. While other countries tend to enjoy the advantages of being **(Q2)** … **(protect)** and are often bailed out of any financial as well as social crisis, these superpowers have to assume higher **(Q3)** … **(responsible)** than ever before.

Recently this **(Q4)** … **(develop)** has caused several countries to consider their actions as well as their impact on other nations. Experts agree that **(Q5)** … **(responsible)** behaviour on any superpower's part could result in problematic or even catastrophic events, for example in terms of the financial world. With the pressure on the more powerful countries **(Q6)** … **(rise)**, they become more and more reluctant to step in and provide support for others, since they feel that they gain nothing but are left with bigger problems. Superpowers often argue that it is unfair that they are expected to take all the blame if anything goes wrong, but **(Q7)** … **(obvious)** lack the influence to make changes before certain problems arise in other countries. At the same time, most countries needing support resent any political **(Q8)** … **(interfere)**, even if they are aware of the fact that they might need help.

KEY

0	*increasingly*	Q5	*irresponsible*
Q1	*globalisation*	Q6	*rising*
Q2	*protected*	Q7	*obviously*
Q3	*responsibilities*	Q8	*interference*
Q4	*development*		

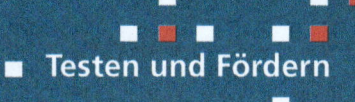
▼18

■ Testen und Fördern

KEY

0 current topics and developments

Q1 conduct theoretical research

Q2 without noticing it/without realising it

Q3 run tests/conduct experiments/carry out experiments

Q4 form bigger blocks/larger blocks

Q5 The environment

Q6 adapts easily/can adapt easily

■ Testen und Fördern

▼18

1. Listening: What did you learn today?

You are going to listen to an interview about learning abilities. First you will have 45 seconds to study the task below, then you will hear the recording twice. While listening, complete the sentences (1–6) using a maximum of four words. Write your answers in the spaces provided. The first one (0) has been done for you. After the second listening you will have 45 seconds to check your answers.

What did you learn today?

0	"Amazing News" focuses on …	*current topics and developments*
Q1	At Coleman's Institute Dr Scott's field of duty is to … .	
Q2	In the future our brain might be able to learn … .	
Q3	In order to find out about people's learning capabilities, the researchers … .	
Q4	When we learn, we combine smaller, individual units to … .	
Q5	… presents the biggest danger to our ability to learn.	
Q6	Our brain can deal with changes in our surroundings, because it … .	

▲18

	the efficiency with which we are learning. In contrary to what we thought all along, our environment might pose the biggest harm to our learning capabilities. Not only do we see increasing proof for the fact that certain kinds of pollution impact our learning skills in a negative way, we have also seen evidence that the abundance of noise and light in our world lead to a decrease in the brain's functions. As a logical conclusion, our surroundings might actually decrease our IQ as well.
	Now this, of course, does not imply that all of us should now react by moving out of the cities to camp out in the desert in order to avoid the dangers of a modern environment. It does, however, point towards the possibility of very real dangers, such as radiation from all types of technical devices. We have absolutely no conclusive knowledge about what the increase in electro-magnetic radiation might do to our bodies and minds. While they might be entirely harmless, we won't be certain of this fact for at least another two decades, when we'll finally be able to observe long-term effects.
	While up to now generations of scientists have seen the solution to any learning problem in technical developments, we now believe that the answer lies in nature itself. Our brain seems to be the organ that adapts most easily to changing conditions, so there is reason to believe that we could coax it to learning by causing it to adapt to new knowledge. The next few years promise to be an exciting time for any researcher and scientist working in this area.
Host	This has been absolutely fascinating. Now, would you ... *(fade out)*

▲18

TAPESCRIPT	
Host	Welcome to this month's feature of our radio show "Amazing News", which, as all of you dedicated listeners know, tries to stay up to date with current topics and developments. This time we are discussing our amazing ability to learn. With me is Dr Thomas Scott, who conducts theoretical research at Coleman's Institute, where he has been making astonishing discoveries about learning and memory. May I welcome you to this show, Dr Scott?
Dr Scott	Why, thank you for inviting me to join you today. It's always a pleasure to present our latest findings to a broader public.
Host	We are happy to have you here. Now, would you like to start us off by giving us an idea of what exactly you are doing at Coleman's Institute and what you have discovered as a result?
Dr Scott	Of course. Well, I would really see our research as ground-breaking, because what we are doing might soon change everything we thought we knew about the way we acquire knowledge. We see a very real possibility to restructure society's ideas about learning due to the fact that right now we are working on techniques to impart knowledge on a brain without it being aware of this process. The realisation of this project lies far ahead in the future, but is becoming more realistic with every day that passes. Right now the employees at Coleman's Institute carry out a series of experiments during which we run tests focusing on our participants' learning capabilities and whether they differ in various parts of their brains.
	Learning is a, um, very complex process, which is influenced by many specific factors, and during which our brains can be entirely rebuilt. What and how we learn determines which areas in our brains are activated and where as well as for how long information is stored. This, in turn, has an impact on how easily we can connect individual pieces of information to form larger blocks. Those blocks form patterns in our minds and can be used to develop and change our knowledge of the world in general.
	The more knowledge we acquire, the more likely it is that our brain increases its learning ability. Of course, there are factors influencing

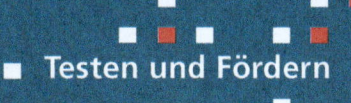

▼19

KEY

0	daughter spending money
Q1	having no credit card
Q2	making minimum payment(s)
Q3	debt accumulates/products become more expensive
Q4	identity theft
Q5	encrypt their information/offer secure payment methods

Testen und Fördern

▼19

2. Listening: Dealing with money

▼ You are going to listen to a discussion between mother and daughter about plastic money. First you will have 45 seconds to study the task below, then you will hear the recording twice. While listening, answer the questions (1–5) using a maximum of four words. Write your answers in the spaces provided. The first one (0) has been done for you. After the second listening you will have 45 seconds to check your answers.

Dealing with money

0	What is the mother complaining about?	*daughter spending money*
Q1	What is meant by "living in medieval times"?	
Q2	Which option do credit cards offer?	
Q3	What happens when the entire credit card bill isn't paid off?	
Q4	What is the biggest danger in others obtaining your bank account information?	
Q5	How do reliable companies protect their customers?	

ōbv © Österreichischer Bundesverlag Schulbuch GmbH & Co. KG, Wien 2014 | Alle Rechte vorbehalten | www.oebv.at | www.testen-und-foerdern.at
Prime Time 8. Testen und Fördern, Arbeitsheft (ISBN 978-3-209-08444-6)

TAPESCRIPT

Mother	Would you mind getting off the computer? All you ever do is spend money you don't have anyways!
Daughter	Oh mum, you are so backward about such things! It's not as if I can't afford it! How can anyone not have a credit card nowadays? I don't understand what is so great about living in medieval times!
Mother	Well, you know, young people always believe that they possess all the wisdom there is. You'll realise that there are one or two things you still have to learn as the years go by! We did not need plastic money back when I was younger, and we do not need it now.
Daughter	Do you even understand the major advantages of being able to purchase products using a card instead of cash? Even if I am lacking the funds to make a purchase at the moment, I can still afford to buy the item and simply cover the bill later that month. Plastic money gives me the flexibility to juggle my finances until for example I receive my paycheck. Every credit card offers me the possibility to make a minimum payment instead of covering the entire sum all at once.
Mother	This is exactly what is wrong with the world today! People live far beyond their means and only realise the risks of this kind of behaviour when they are too far in debt. Paying a minimum fee simply means that your debt with the credit card company accumulates and the price of the originally purchased product increases. In addition, there is the danger of becoming unaware of what your actual debt amounts to. Remember, you frequently make use of several cards, which also means that the interest you pay on each of them adds up.
Daughter	You would think I am entirely irresponsible when it comes to my personal finances. With the new and improved online banking system my bank offers, I am always aware of each card's balance and limits. That is another point, right there. Online banking provides me with the opportunity to take care of any financial business 24/7. So I am actually saving money by not having to enter an actual bank to take care of transactions.

Mother	Don't you worry about this online banking system being prone to manipulation? I have recently watched a documentary on identity theft due to bank account information being stolen. When that happens, you could be driven into financial ruin, or run into problems with the law, especially if your identity is used to commit crimes. Are there even ways to ensure that this can't happen to you?
Daughter	Well, of course I always conduct business with well-known companies offering secure methods of payment and utilising sites which encrypt the customer's information so it cannot be hacked. There is certainly some risk involved, but everybody is doing it and you would have to have really bad luck to be the person affected. Credit card companies even offer an insurance against the theft and misuse of their cards, so customers will not be greatly impacted if something like that did happen.
Mother	All I know is that if you look at the state of most societies today, there is an enormous rise in the number of people who will never be able to pay off their debts. Much of this is caused by the careless usage of plastic money. Young people in particular seem to live by the rule "Purchase today, pay tomorrow". I just hope you won't get yourself in a situation like that … (fade out)

▲19

▲19

3. Reading: Why scientists could easily be ruling the world

Read the text below, then choose the correct answer (A, B, C or D) for questions 1–5. Put a ☒ in the correct box. The first one (0) has been done for you.

Why scientists could easily be ruling the world

Abortion is an extremely controversial topic in the United States with both sides of the debate duelling it out over what is right or wrong. The law presently controlling abortion in America was introduced in 1973 by the Supreme Court. According to this law, women have the right to choose how they want to handle a pregnancy, whether through termination or continuation. Since this court ruling, abortion has been in the national spotlight and the centre of the debate still remains whether it should actually still be legal or overturned.

Before this ruling there had been abortion laws in the US as early as the 1820s. However, by 1900 most abortions had been outlawed because of the extreme pressure from the American Medical Association, physicians and legislators. Nevertheless, this did not prevent illegal abortions, which at the time were a dangerous practice, from taking place. The main difference was that women did not only risk their lives due to the bad hygienic conditions under which such procedures took place, but also because few abortions were carried out by medical professionals any more. By 1965, all states had banned abortions altogether, with few exceptions being allowed. Finally, abortion was once again legalised in 1973 in all fifty states, using a trimester framework that freed doctors to perform abortions for any reason in the first trimester and giving the individual states the power to regulate the second and third trimester. In the years since this decision many pro-life groups, such as the Human Life Foundation or the Life Coalition, have been formed which have taken up the fight against this ruling and presented alternatives such as adoption. They have been the driving forces behind new restrictions and regulations that have been introduced, such as required parental consent for teenagers. These pro-life organisations arrange many protests and lobby to bring forth legislation to end the age-old debate of how to handle an unexpected pregnancy. Often, these groups see the practice of abortion as an unlawful procedure that takes a defenseless human life and advocate adoption as the only legal alternative. Furthermore, they argue that life begins at conception, whereas the other side of the debate believes that no rights other than those stated in the Constitution should be judicially recognised and protected.

There are many different reasons why a woman might decide to have an abortion. If there are irreparable defects concerning the fetus, such as major development failures or problems with the heart, nervous system, brain, kidneys or breathing system, a woman might choose to end the pregnancy. There are other common reasons that a woman might choose to have an abortion such as birth control failure, unwanted or unplanned pregnancy, not being able to support or provide for the child or medical conditions that could seriously endanger the woman's health. Most women concerned choose to abort based on their current needs, feelings and economic position. Especially women aged between 15 and 20 often do not feel prepared to take responsibility for another human being. They might lack sufficient means to provide for themselves and a child. Unfinished education and lack of mental maturity are factors that particularly cause young females to abort. However, younger women are not the only ones making such drastic decisions, which may have a strong impact on their future lives. Research shows that abortions are no longer limited to a certain age group of women.

On average, one million women in the US decide to abort their unborn children every year. This decision, which is often made in a moment of desperation or panic, may cause inner turmoil and stress. No matter whether having an abortion is legal or not, in the end it is always the woman who has to deal with the choice she has made.

ōbv © Österreichischer Bundesverlag Schulbuch GmbH & Co. KG, Wien 2014 | Alle Rechte vorbehalten | www.oebv.at | www.testen-und-foerdern.at
Prime Time 8. Testen und Fördern, Arbeitsheft (ISBN 978-3-209-08444-6)

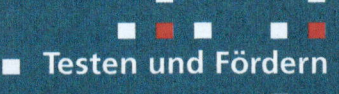
▲22

KEY

0–B
Q1–C
Q2–B
Q3–C
Q4–D
Q5–D

legalised abortion.
a rise in the practice of illegal abortion.
allowed abortion throughout the US.
stricter regulations on abortion.
educational background.
to explain the background of abortion

▲22

0 The 1973 law
A banned abortion. ☐
B legalised abortion. ☒
C led to a protest. ☐
D was overturned. ☐

Q1 Banning abortion around 1900 caused
A a lot of pressure from doctors and lawyers. ☐
B an increase in death following abortion. ☐
C a rise in the practice of illegal abortion. ☐
D a decrease of medical professionals. ☐

Q2 Regulations on abortion after 1973
A allowed abortion up to the second trimester. ☐
B allowed abortion throughout the US. ☐
C banned abortion after the second trimester. ☐
D banned abortion in individual states. ☐

Q3 The formation of pro-life groups resulted in
A stronger support for single mothers. ☐
B the creation of educational programmes. ☐
C stricter regulations on abortion. ☐
D a ban on teenage abortion. ☐

Q4 The main reason for teenage girls to abort is their
A psychological stability. ☐
B physical maturity. ☐
C financial situation. ☐
D educational background. ☐

Q5 What is the purpose of the text?
A to criticise women who abort ☐
B to illustrate the dangers of abortion ☐
C to argue a ban on abortion ☐
D to explain the background of abortion ☐

öbv © Österreichischer Bundesverlag Schulbuch GmbH & Co. KG, Wien 2014 | Alle Rechte vorbehalten | www.oebv.at | www.testen-und-foerdern.at
Prime Time 8. Testen und Fördern, Arbeitsheft (ISBN 978-3-209-08444-6)
76

4. Reading: The newspaper of the future

Read the text below. Parts of the text have been removed. Choose the correct part (A–I) for the gaps (1–6). There are two extra parts you should not use. Write your answers in the boxes provided. The first one (0) has been done for you.

The newspaper of the future

Ever since the invention of printing methods effective enough to **(0)** … , a printed version of the latest news has been a consistent and reliable part of our lives. We even got used to **(Q1)** … and to be aware as well as warned of right to our front door, ever since a system for subscription and delivery was introduced.

For a few years now, however, it seemed as if this precious part of our society was on a fast decrease, due to its own reinvention on the internet. People aged between 15 and 30 in particular admit to **(Q2)** … to all kinds of news online and even point out the benefit of being able to compare and contrast different sources before making up their mind about certain events. Furthermore, appealing features such as live feeds and supporting video material add to the belief that online newspapers present the reader with a much more wholesome picture of what is happening around the globe than traditional papers ever could.

So why should we even mourn the slow death of the traditional newspaper? In terms of immediate accessibility, faster spreading of current events and availability of further information it seems at a clear disadvantage when **(Q3)** … . It is also more costly, more prone to being impacted by catastrophic events due to possible difficulties in production, and much less extensive in terms of the information it provides. There are, however, quite a few points **(Q4)** … .

While online versions claim their vast amount of information as a benefit, readers can easily be overwhelmed by the sheer number of articles available to them on certain topics. They might become side-tracked and actually restrict their own view because they rarely take the time to sort through all the topics of the day. Thus, online readers tend to focus on specific areas of interest but neglect even skimming over anything else. This is made possible because every online version contains a search link **(Q5)** … where they want to go.

Due to the speed news are spreading with, online papers can easily become a perfect platform for exaggeration as well as hysteria and consequently the source of panic among the masses. Even smaller events which might not have been **(Q6)** … a few decades back now lead to lengthy discussions and unnecessary fear among citizens. While there are quite a few beneficial aspects to the reduction in time news need to spread, such as quicker responses of rescue teams and charity organisations to disasters or catastrophes, there are obviously also drawbacks to this development.

Nevertheless, latest trends point towards new and improved combinations of both, printed as well as online newspapers, which might enable future readers to enjoy the best of both worlds.

A	relying entirely on having access
B	introduced to the audience
C	compared to online versions
D	explaining the disadvantage of newspapers
E	produce books and newspaper for the masses
F	taken all that seriously
G	defending the importance of the traditional newspaper
H	having all we ever needed to know
I	enabling the audience to get directly to

KEY

0	Q1	Q2	Q3	Q4	Q5	Q6
E	H	A	C	G	I	F

KEY

0	Q1	Q2	Q3	Q4	Q5	Q6	Q7	Q8	Q9	Q10	Q11
K	A	J	F	B	M	E	N	I	D	G	C

▲25

---

5. Language in use: Should more fathers be spending time with their children?

You are going to read a text about men staying at home with their children. Some words are missing from the text. Choose from the list (A–N) the correct part for each gap (1–11) in the text. There are two extra words you should not use. Write your answers in the boxes provided. The first one (0) has been done for you.

Should more fathers be spending time with their children?

The current discussion **(0)** … around why fathers are often still very reluctant to be a stay-at-home dad has shown that most of them feel that their profession does not **(Q1)** … for such a decision. Even though over 50 per cent of men claimed that they would like to have the possibility of **(Q2)** … their children for some time, very few fathers take the actual step. In many cases they feel intimidated due to the doubts being **(Q3)** … by their work environment if they will be able to juggle their career while **(Q4)** … up their children at the same time. Although mothers have been **(Q5)** … with the very same problem for decades, the world does not seem to be entirely ready for fathers to take on this new role. Apart from the fact that many companies are not yet **(Q6)** … with child care facilities and much less offer proper part-time employment opportunities, there are still strong tendencies in society towards **(Q7)** … the mother as the proper caretaker of a small child. Nevertheless, laws have been **(Q8)** … by many governments which **(Q9)** … both partners to equally share the time they spend with their children. Therefore, the main problem seems to lie in the fact that men often **(Q10)** … ridicule by their peers should they decide to **(Q11)** … their children over their careers.

A allow	**E** equipped	**I** passed	**M** struggling
B bringing	**F** expressed	**J** raising	**N** viewing
C choose	**G** face	~~**K** revolving~~	
D enable	**H** invented	**L** rising	

▲25

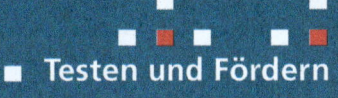

6. Language in use: Going virtual

You are going to read a text about virtual life. Some words are missing from the text. Choose the correct answer (A, B, C or D) for each gap (1–7) in the text. Write your answers in the boxes provided. The first one (0) has been done for you.

Going virtual

(0) ... studies have shown that there might be numerous benefits to spending time in a virtual world, provided that the person **(Q1)** ... does not lose touch with reality. Experts in brain development **(Q2)** ... have discovered that people deal better with many real-life scenarios if they have gone over them in their minds repeatedly. Thus, spending some time in a virtual reality could result in an increase in a person's actual **(Q3)** ..., such as better sportsmanship or improved social skills.

Thus, psychiatrists as well as therapists have started to reap the **(Q4)** ... of the multitude of available scenarios the virtual world offers. Their patients can face fears and phobias, while knowing that they are perfectly safe and therefore practice taking different **(Q5)** ... to problematic situations. The more frequently they are introduced to such forms of therapy, the more comfortable they become with similar situations in real life.

Furthermore, this technology has been adopted by universities and other educational institutions in order to prepare their students for worldly scenarios they will **(Q6)** ... in their professional lives. This includes business meetings, giving speeches in front of crowds, conflict management, and negotiations. By **(Q7)** ... their students with in-depth training, schools believe that they can ensure a more capable and efficient generation of future employees or employers.

	A	B	C	D
0	Recent	Latest	Modern	Contemporary
Q1	A involved	convoluted	affected	concerned
Q2	A study	research	investigation	exploration
Q3	A abilities	facilities	aptitudes	capacities
Q4	A aids	paybacks	benefits	assistances
Q5	A tactics	approaches	attitudes	methods
Q6	A come upon	bump into	struggle	encounter
Q7	A offering	showing	providing	obtaining

KEY

0	Q1	Q2	Q3	Q4	Q5	Q6	Q7
A	D	B	A	C	B	D	C

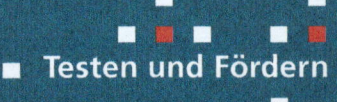
▼34

Testen und Fördern

Q3 What is problematic about the newly evolving form of "individualism"?

A Responsibility towards society ceases to exist. ☐

B Unacceptable behaviour occurs among individualists. ☐

C Individualism becomes a private lifestyle. ☐

D Individualism interferes with our social duties. ☐

Q4 Recent developments around the world point towards other

A a lack of responsibility towards other ☐

B a rise in the number of individualists ☐

C an increase in criminal activity ☐

D a decrease in recklessness among individualists ☐

Q5 According to Mr Janks, what danger are we already facing?

A falling into anarchy ☐

B loss of all established rules ☐

C destruction of society ☐

D irreversible consequences ☐

▼33

Testen und Fördern

1. Listening: The conflict of individualism

▼ You are going to listen to an interview about the conflict of individualism. First you will have 45 seconds to study the task below, then you will hear the recording twice. While listening, choose the correct answer (A, B, C or D) for questions 1–5. Put a ☒ in the correct box. The first one (0) has been done for you. After the second listening you will have 45 seconds to check your answers.

The conflict of individualism

0 How often does this radio show air?

A every week ☐

B every two weeks ☒

C twice a week ☐

D once a month ☐

Q1 Mr Janks' interest in the topic was raised by

A the enormous changes he observed. ☐

B the widening gap between society and individual. ☐

C the growing freedom of individuals. ☐

D the implications of an increase in individualism. ☐

Q2 What did the term "individualism" express in former times?

A the ability to go beyond society's limits ☐

B the individual's functions in society ☐

C the perception of our private lives ☐

D the difference between people in society and as an individual ☐

KEY

0–B   every two weeks
Q1–B   the widening gap between society and individual.
Q2–A   the ability to go beyond society's limits
Q3–D   Individualism interferes with our social duties.
Q4–A   a lack of responsibility towards other
Q5–C   destruction of society

TAPESCRIPT

Host	Welcome to all the bookworms out there for today's interview with famous author Timothy Janks, with whom we will discuss his latest bestseller *The conflict of individualism*. Mr Janks, may I welcome you to our show "Literary news", which informs interested readers biweekly about current must-haves in the world of books.
Timothy Janks	Thank you! I have been looking forward to being here. You know, this is my first time on a radio show and I have been feeling quite nervous. While I seem to be able to write decent books, I have been told that my voice is not the most pleasant sound in the world.
Host	We have a lot of guests who feel uncomfortable about hearing their own voice on the air, but believe me, it is never as bad as you fear it is going to be. Now, from what I hear your book has been hitting the bestseller lists once again. Would you mind explaining what your latest work focuses on?
Timothy Janks	Well, I have actually tried to cover a variety of topics I have been noticing over the past few years. My field of study is behavioural analysis and I must admit that I see profound changes occurring in society. The growing conflict between mankind living in a society and individuals claiming increasing freedom to determine their own lifestyle was what first caused me to research this issue in more detail. Thus, I looked at what a sharp rise in individualism could imply for all of mankind today as well as for future generations.
Host	Since you have already mentioned a key concept explained in your book, what exactly are you referring to when discussing the term "individualism"?
Timothy Janks	Uhm, as I outline there, it is my belief that the term has recently undergone some changes. Before, it merely referred to the fact that every one of us always differentiated between the function we fulfilled in society and the individual we perceived ourselves to be in our private lives. Individualism was nothing more than a term coined for a concept, which enabled us to break free of certain boundaries set by society. Today, however, there is increasing evidence, that the free choice to go beyond limits is ranked higher than the responsibility towards society. In other words, since individualism gradually ceases to be an alternative private lifestyle, there is the possible consequence that extreme individualists will stop performing their social functions. This effect could easily lead to a disruption of the unwritten sets of rules every society has and expects its members to behave accordingly to.
Host	But haven't there always been members in any society who would not play by the rules?
Timothy Janks	Oh, of course, and that fact in itself would not provide us with any bigger problems than we had so far. However, what we see occurring now across the globe is a growing amount of recklessness in terms of the consequences their behaviour might have on the lives of others. To a certain extent I point out in my book that this could have been caused by the typical characteristics of the modern media, which allow for us to be anonymous perpetrators who do not have to accept responsibility in the same way the real world demands. This fact could prompt people to take actions they would commonly shy away from. Most recent proof of this fact is the emergence of cyber-bullying among even young schoolchildren. When I speak of individualism today, I refer first and foremost to a form of selfishness that – if ever spinning out of control – poses a danger to all the rules we have established in society and whose consequences might even be irreversible. I am not saying that we are on the brink of anarchy, but we have turned our steps down a quite dangerous road by allowing this trend to push us towards destruction of society as we know it.
Host	So how do you think this process could be stopped or even reversed?
Timothy Janks	Clearly, we have to spread awareness of this development, so people take a close look at their actions and their consequences. As a second step, it will be necessary that we increase pressure to accept their share of responsibility on the people concerned. As for reversing the process, … *(fade out)*

ōbv © Österreichischer Bundesverlag Schulbuch GmbH & Co. KG, Wien 2014 | Alle Rechte vorbehalten | www.oebv.at | www.testen-und-foerdern.at
Prime Time 8. Testen und Fördern, Arbeitsheft (ISBN 978-3-209-08444-6)

Lösungen section

▼35

KEY

0	globalisation and its effects
Q1	her alma mater/university/Berkeley
Q2	major incidents/wars/personal catastrophic events
Q3	add aspects to/enhance/complete
Q4	satisfied we are/we perceive the situation/we see our nation
Q5	differing living standards/envy/jealousy (towards other nations)
Q6	censorship/restrictive laws

TAPESCRIPT

Interviewer	Can we get started?
Prof Storms	Professor Storms, thank for meeting with me today. Since you have kindly agreed to answer some of mine and our listeners' burning questions on globalisation and its effects, would you give our audience an idea of how you became an expert on this topic?
Prof Storms	Uhm, well, after finishing my studies in International Management at Berkeley University, I accepted the position of assistant manager for a multinational company where I had to deal with the latest developments in globalisation on a daily basis and for the duration of almost seven years. From there, my career led me back to my alma mater, where I became a professor in the International Management Department. This position enabled me to intensify my research concerning the effects of globalisation on national identities and to publish a series of articles as well as a book on this topic.
Interviewer	Before we move on to the effects, could you explain the term "national identity" to our listeners?
Prof Storms	Certainly. As all of us know, every person develops their own identity in the course of their lives, which they usually stick to, unless some major incident forces them to adapt to a changing environment. Such incidents could be wars, or personal catastrophic events. Now, apart from that, people also perceive themselves as belonging to a nation, which adds different aspects to their personal identity. We might even say that one is not complete without the other. Those aspects are somewhat similar among all the members of a nation and usually include at least one common language, a set of beliefs, morals and values, and a system of traditions and behavioural patterns. All of those factors together form what we call a national identity.

Test page section

2. Listening: Does globalisation threaten our national identity?

You are going to listen to an interview about globalisation and national identity. First you will have 45 seconds to study the task below, then you will hear the recording twice. While listening, complete the sentences (1–6) using a maximum of four words. Write your answers in the spaces provided. The first one (0) has been done for you. After the second listening you will have 45 seconds to check your answers.

Does globalisation threaten our national identity?

0	Professor Storms is an expert on … .	globalisation and its effects
Q1	After working for a multinational company, Professor Storms returned to … .	
Q2	Personal identities remain stagnant except for the occurrence of … .	
Q3	People's national identities … their personal identities.	
Q4	Global factors have an influence on how … .	
Q5	Protest among citizens is usually caused by … .	
Q6	Citizens are less supportive of countries which make use of … .	

▼35

3. Reading: The misery of illegal aliens

Read the text below, then choose the correct answer (A, B, C or D) for questions 1–5.

Put a ☒ in the correct box. The first one (0) has been done for you.

The misery of illegal aliens

Ever since the gap between industrialised and developing countries has become so wide, there has been an increase in illegal immigration into the countries that are economically better off. It could be argued that travelling to or staying in another state illegally is a mistake to begin with, since it leaves the immigrants with a lot of problems. However, thousands of people have little to no chance to be accepted as a legal immigrant or to be given a visa for economic reasons. This forces many of them to use alternative ways which might be illegal, but at least seems to provide them with the chance to achieve their ultimate goal of leaving their home country and settling down in a country which might offer a job and even a small, regular income.

Apart from the seemingly ample benefits, many so-called illegal aliens face a whole myriad of problems once they arrive at their destination. Not only do they live in fear of being discovered and deported back to their country of origin, in the most extreme cases there is even the danger of being imprisoned. Reoccurring illegal migrating activities may lead to serious legal charges. Furthermore, on a daily basis there are all kinds of difficulties, especially when dealing with the authorities.

Unlike normal citizens, illegal immigrants have trouble obtaining any type of legal document or performing legal actions, such as getting a local driver's licence or registering a car in their name. Since they do not exist in a legal sense, small obstacles in their way towards a better existence and standard of living can easily become insurmountable difficulties. Another very real consequence of having no permit to stay in a country is the fact that illegal aliens are often subject to exploitation.

Due to their problematic status, there is little to no protection against people who are trying to use illegal immigrants to their own advantage. If they manage to find accommodation, for example, there is no guarantee that the landlord will treat them in a fair way. They might be thrown out without a warning or be forced to pay much higher rent than usual. Although local people often argue that the problem lies in the language barrier or the difference in culture, the underlying fact is a different one. Illegal immigrants are dependent on the mercy of other people and have no possibility to take any legal action towards people who exploit them or treat them inappropriately.

Apart from possible mistreatment, there is another major drawback to crossing boarders illegally. After their initial arrival many illegal immigrants become aware of the fact that they

Interviewer	I can honestly say that I have never thought about my identity that way. It is a fascinating topic. Now, in how far can globalisation then have an impact on this form of identity?
Prof Storms	Well, to begin with, globalisation affects almost every area of our lives, whether we are aware of this fact or not. Some of these factors, however, determine how we perceive our nation's status quo and whether we are satisfied with it. For example, living standards may vary considerably among different nations, which can easily leave one nation's citizens in uproar, especially if the situation is believed to have been caused by bad decisions made by the ones in charge. Other areas which are commonly subject to envy and jealousy are the availability of products or the existence of social support systems. When we reach a point where the majority of citizens experiences the present situation as unbearable, loyalty towards their nation decreases and consequently threatens the unquestioned existence of their national identity.
Interviewer	Assuming this is the case, what consequences would this nation have to face?
Prof Storms	That depends on several factors. In general it must be said that countries offering more benefits in form of monetary support or unemployment programmes suffer less from periods of disappointment or protest among their citizens. In contrast to that, nations which tend to tightly control their citizens' personal freedom, may it be through censorship or restrictive laws, are in a bigger danger of losing public support.
Interviewer	If support for their own nations vanishes, where do people turn to, then?
Prof Storms	What we have seen in the past few years is that globalisation has turned an increasing number of people into "global identities", who feel no longer tied to a certain nation, but embrace the concept of belonging to a global mega-society. While this society is still developing its own moral codes and basic beliefs, more and more people see the benefits in being able to develop an interconnected global nation.
Interviewer	Thank you very much, Professor Storm, for your explanations on this topic. Now let's see what questions are on our listener's minds … (fade out)

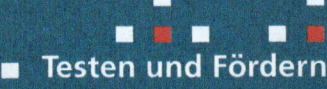

▼37

might have robbed themselves of any way to ever return to their home country in a legal way. The reason for that is the problem of obtaining a permit to stay once you have entered the country illegally. Most countries are determined to withhold such benefits from persons who never had an official permission to immigrate, which prevents many illegal immigrants from applying for a visa in the first place. Thus, illegal immigrants might never be able to leave their chosen destination again. Without proof of being a legal immigrant, they would be stopped at the boarder or at any airport when trying to travel and would be taken in for questioning. Most likely they would never be allowed to return after facing the usual consequence of being deported back to their home country. Since most people refrain from facing such a risk, they do not travel outside of their new home country.

Finally, employment and health care are also very problematic for those people. Naturally, nobody will be able to employ them officially, so they are stuck with low-skill jobs that are commonly badly paid. Most well-paid jobs require legal documents and proof of education, which are hard to get in this situation. Without a working permit, however, there will be no health benefits that typically come with a stable job. Since the majority of people do not make enough money to afford private insurance, this usually results in little or no health care. Living ever day in fear of falling ill is reality for many illegal immigrants.

0 Illegal immigration is high in countries which

- A offer better economic circumstances. ☒
- B are developing into rich nations. ☐
- C are politically rather stable. ☐
- D offer easy ways of immigration. ☐

Q1 Most of these immigrants make the decision to do so illegally, because

- A they have no income in their home country. ☐
- B they expect a higher living standard. ☐
- C they have run out of alternative ways. ☐
- D they believe they have no legal chance. ☐

▼38

Q2 Illegal immigrants may be put into jail, if

- A they are to be deported back to their country of origin. ☐
- B they are found to immigrate without permission repeatedly. ☐
- C they are forced to deal with the authorities ☐
- D they are involved in other criminal activities. ☐

Q3 Because of their illegal situation, many immigrants

- A lose their driver's licence. ☐
- B cannot buy a new car. ☐
- C depend on other people's trust. ☐
- D cannot get a new passport. ☐

Q4 Often such immigrants run into problems with landlords, because

- A they cannot pay the rent. ☐
- B they do not speak the local language. ☐
- C they cannot take others to court. ☐
- D they misunderstand the local culture. ☐

Q5 Illegal immigrants' fear to apply for an official visa is caused by

- A the government's refusal to grant them. ☐
- B the restrictions on travelling back home. ☐
- C the threat of deportation through boarder control. ☐
- D the costs for such an official document. ☐

KEY

- 0–A offer better economic circumstances.
- Q1–D they believe they have no legal chance.
- Q2–B they are found to immigrate without permission repeatedly.
- Q3–D cannot get a new passport.
- Q4–C they cannot take others to court.
- Q5–A the government's reluctance to grant them.

öbv © Österreichischer Bundesverlag Schulbuch GmbH & Co. KG, Wien 2014 | Alle Rechte vorbehalten | www.oebv.at | www.testen-und-foerdern.at
Prime Time 8. Testen und Fördern, Arbeitsheft (ISBN 978-3-209-08444-6)

4. Reading: Peace – Mission Impossible?

Read the text below, then answer the questions (1–6) using a maximum of four words. Write your answers in the spaces provided. The first one (0) has been done for you.

Peace – Mission Impossible?

Although the world has seen two World Wars and suffered the consequences of such major events, humankind appears to have learned little about how to live in peace with each other. There are still many unresolved conflicts with the potential of drawing many other countries into them as well. Due to alliances and organisations binding several countries together, political statements and actions have to be watched closely, since they might not only trigger the reaction of the country attacked or insulted, but also of several others.

Nevertheless, many wars in the past have taught us some important lessons about the extreme losses resulting from military conflicts. We can still vividly remember pictures of destroyed buildings, injured or dead soldiers as well as civilians, and half-starved children. It is usually the normal population who suffer most from wars. Apart from the fact that many fall victim to attacks, the economy of the country concerned often comes to a screeching halt. This results in high unemployment rates, inflation and lack of resources, such as food or energy. In addition, it can take the economy years to recover from the decrease in industry and production as well as the destruction of infrastructure.

With all those factors in mind, it seems to be obvious that keeping peace should be the top priority of any government. Not only are there extensive economic benefits, since multinational companies tend to choose peaceful countries as headquarters and to run main operations in, but there is first and foremost a climate of political stability. People who live in peaceful times tend to appreciate their government and politicians more and are also willing to support the political system they live in. In addition, they are more productive, because they profit from their own hard work and manage to establish a higher standard of living.

Thus, the questions remains, why countries decide against peace, if there are so many clear advantages to it. One determining factor why countries enter into military conflict is political reasons. In cases where the population is suppressed by a military regime or a dictatorship, other countries might decide to spring into action in order to enforce a more stable system. Whether this is the right way to deal with such situations is questionable. Especially when a country suffers from civil war, soldiers from other countries are often sent in to stop the violence. On the other hand, frequent violations of human rights through governments such as torture, censorship or unjustified imprisonment are also often the cause for arising conflicts, which are usually following an international outcry.

Nevertheless, the main problem with an ideal world living in peace lies in the character of human beings. Although we possess a certain control over our feelings, aggression is still among our basic instinctive reactions. Whenever we feel insulted or attacked, our initial urge goes towards using violence for protection and defence. Even though we realise that this desire might be misplaced and might not go through with it, keeping the peace might be more difficult for us than one might hope.

0	What threatens peace today?	unresolved conflicts
Q1	Who might react to political insults or activities?	
Q2	In terms of financial matters, what do wars often result in?	
Q3	What has to be increased in order to reverse the effects of war?	
Q4	What is the main benefit of peace?	
Q5	According to the author, what reason might rightfully cause a conflict?	
Q6	How do people react to provocation?	

KEY

0	unresolved conflicts
Q1	countries and their allies/several countries
Q2	loss of money value/inflation
Q3	industry and production/infrastructure
Q4	political stability/politically stable climate
Q5	violations of human rights
Q6	they protect themselves/they defend themselves/desire for violence/aggression

Testen und Fördern

▼41

KEY

0	majority
Q1	treatment
Q2	safety
Q3	economically
Q4	unemployment
Q5	focused
Q6	personalities
Q7	reflection
Q8	consideration
Q9	underestimate

Testen und Fördern

▼41

5. Language in use: Do our own needs surpass our compassion for others?

You are going to read a text about needs. Some words are missing from the text. Use the word in brackets to complete each gap (1–9). Write your answers in the spaces provided at the end of the text. The first one (0) has been done for you.

Do our own needs surpass our compassion for others?

Unlike centuries ago, the **(0)** … **(major)** of people in our society today enjoy a life where their most basic needs, such as a place to live, food and medical **(Q1)** … **(treat)** are covered. Due to the quite extensive **(Q2)** … **(safe)** net most western states offer, even people in potentially **(Q3)** … **(economy)** difficult situations such as **(Q4)** … **(employ)**, or health problems are usually provided with enough financial means to live on. As a consequence, our priorities in terms of desires seem to have shifted. The more security we have in life, the more **(Q5)** … **(focus)** we become on more elaborate desires, such as a successful professional life, or happy personal relationships.

However, in recent years our personal needs tend to emphasise our desire to develop our **(Q6)** … **(personal)** as well as to evaluate our own progress. First and foremost, our world revolves around ourselves. Instead of broadening our horizon, we concentrate on **(Q7)** … **(reflect)**, meditation and self-development. Searching for our inner god or goddess has become the ultimate goal in terms of personal development. While this is not necessarily negative, the focus we put on ourselves might lead to a lack of **(Q8)** … **(consider)** and compassion for the people around us. While it might be important to be concerned with ourselves every now and then, we should never **(Q9)** … **(estimate)** the value of love and friendship as well as the joy it brings to support others in fulfilling their dreams.

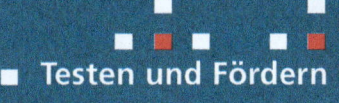
▲43

6. Language in use: Is there still an American Dream?

You are going to read a text about the American Dream. Some words are missing from the text. Choose the correct answer (A, B, C or D) for each gap (1–10) in the text. Write your answers in the boxes provided. The first one (0) has been done for you.

Is there still an American Dream?

The American Dream represents the ideal life most Americans desire, including an amazing job with a high **(0)** .... a perfect little family and a nice home. Only a few decades ago thousands of families in America lived an almost perfect life in **(Q1)** .... and with seemingly endless great opportunities. Unfortunately, the times when it was rather easy to go from rags to **(Q2)** ... seem to be over. In times of economic **(Q3)** ... it has become much harder to hold on to a job or save up a little money, let alone acquire enough wealth to make bigger **(Q4)** .... such as property. Many people are even **(Q5)** ... to afford health insurance for their family or to fix broken **(Q6)** ... around the house.

In addition, many private households have **(Q7)** ... high amounts of debt, which in turn makes it impossible for them to pay their everyday bills in the long run. This situation has been caused by the development of a society made up of consumers who are used to having everything at their beck and call at any time a day. **(Q8)** ... out credits and loans can therefore be seen as a result of the desire to **(Q9)** ... a high standard of living, even though the **(Q10)** ... circumstances have changed entirely. In contrast to the abundant wealth the American society was used to they will have to move on to a time of saving and dreaming on a smaller scale.

▲42

	A	B	C	D
0	✗ income	payment	profits	returns
Q1	A riches	B prosperity	C affluence	D opulence
Q2	A richer	B riches	C rich	D richest
Q3	A collapse	B boom	C recession	D prosperity
Q4	A purchases	B purchasing	C gains	D gaining
Q5	A struggling	B managing	C succeeding	D harassing
Q6	A applications	B designs	C appliances	D goods
Q7	A gathered	B increased	C hoarded	D accumulated
Q8	A taking	B getting	C borrowing	D lending
Q9	A retain	B maintain	C sustain	D contain
Q10	A ergonomical	B ecological	C economical	D economic

KEY

0	Q1	Q2	Q3	Q4	Q5	Q6	Q7	Q8	Q9	Q10
A	B	B	C	A	A	A	C	D	A	B	A	D

▼49

KEY

0	successful authors
Q1	shares his secret(s)
Q2	explore the unknown/go beyond limits
Q3	see every facet/aspect
Q4	approach
Q5	periods of no/zero creativity

▼49

1. Listening: The secret of writing a book

▼ You are going to listen to a lecture on the secret behind writing successful books. First you will have 45 seconds to study the task below, then you will hear the recording twice. While listening, complete the sentences (1–5) using a maximum of four words. Write your answers in the spaces provided. The first one (0) has been done for you. After the second listening you will have 45 seconds to check your answers.

The secret of writing a book

0	Matthew Hamilton promises the participants of his seminar to become ...	*successful authors*
Q1	According to Hamilton, he differs from other authors because he	
Q2	Creating a storyline for a book is fascinating, because you are free to	
Q3	The technique the author uses to create characters allows him to	
Q4	New authors have to choose their own ... to writing a book.	
Q5	Hamilton admits to having	

▶49

day they can be found at their keyboard typing along at precisely 9 a.m. and they will switch off their computers at 5 p.m. sharp. For those of you not able yet to afford the luxury of writing books as their only profession, it might be a good idea to decide on a time frame of one or two hours a day when you will sit down and write. For myself, however, time frames have never worked all that well, which is why I suffer from long periods of absolutely zero creativity interrupted by short episodes of desperate writing, during which I might produce an entire book. If I'm lucky, my editor even thinks it might be worth selling.

Like most authors I have also lived through the terrifying moments, hours or even months of writer's block. Now this is difficult to deal with ... *(fade out)*

▶49

TAPESCRIPT

Good evening, ladies and gentlemen. Thank you all for taking part in my seminar "The secret behind writing books". My name is Matthew Hamilton and I am the author of Why writing does not have to be as difficult as it sounds. After tonight, you will possess the knowledge on how to write a successful book, utilising all the talents hidden inside of you. Now, before we start, I want you to remember, that there are many authors out there who would never dream of sharing their work processes with you. Fortunately for you, however, I simply can't keep a secret.

To begin with, any successful book is based on a great story with elaborate characters. Determining where your book's plot is going to lead you is one of the most exciting aspects of being an author. While you are creating an image of this entirely new world, you can go above and beyond any limit. There is virtually nothing stopping you or holding you back, since you enjoy the ultimate freedom of exploring the unknown. In many cases you will discover that plot and characters alike take on a life of their own and begin to guide you to where they want to go. While you generally feel more in control in the beginning of the writing process, the storyline starts to almost write itself the closer you get to the end. I have often caught myself being surprised at the twists and turns my plots took. Sometimes it seemed as if some stranger had taken my place. Nevertheless, there is a certain magic to letting your own phantasy run wild.

When it comes to designing well-rounded and believable characters, I have found that I needed to acquire in-depth knowledge about them long before I ever tried to tell their stories. There is a technique I usually apply in order to develop my protagonists. By playing out their entire lives from the second of their birth to their last breath, I can create an image in my mind which shows me every single facet before I have to put one word down on paper. Frequently I feel as if I know my characters better than I could ever know myself, because they hold no surprises for me.

Now let's move on to the most mysterious part of an author's work process: how he or she actually goes about writing books. There are as many approaches as there are authors and it will be up to you to determine the one that will enable you to produce great literary works. Nevertheless, let's take a look at several options you could start out with. Now, I can think of several colleagues who draw up a work schedule to which they stick religiously. Each

▲50

KEY

0–E	giving an overview of today's topics.
Q1–C	becoming increasingly different.
Q2–F	being developed.
Q3–G	being insecure and disoriented.
Q4–A	becoming more aware of the situation.
Q5–D	being even unhappier.

▲50

2. Listening: The biggest lies about beauty

You are going to listen to a recording about the biggest lies about beauty. First you will have 45 seconds to study the task below, then you will hear the recording twice. While listening, match the beginnings of the sentences (1–5) with the sentence endings (A–H). There are two extra sentence endings you should not use. Write your answers in the spaces provided. The first one (0) has been done for you. After the second listening you will have 45 seconds to check your answers.

The biggest lies about beauty

		E
0	The radio host starts out by …	
Q1	People around the world and their ideas on beauty are …	
Q2	Young adults' images of beauty are …	
Q3	The conflict between realistic views and society's requirements results in people …	
Q4	In their everyday lives, people can't avoid …	
Q5	For most patients, cosmetic surgery results in …	

A	… becoming more aware of the situation.
B	… adapting to recent changes.
C	… becoming increasingly different.
D	… being even unhappier.
E	… giving an overview of today's topics.
F	… being developed.
G	… being insecure and disoriented.
H	… being adapted.

öbv

TAPESCRIPT

Mitch Lane	Hello to all you listeners out there and welcome to another afternoon full of interesting news, fascinating facts and amazing reports! This is Mitch Lane and you are listening to this week's broadcast of "Haven't you heard?". As always, let me give you a quick overview of today's topics. First on our list is a short report on the biggest lies about beauty, followed by some of the latest gossip about your favourite celebrities, and finally we will provide you with ten awesome ways to save money. Now, the following report has been released by a research team at Cambridge and offers truly remarkable insights into the topic of beauty. Enjoy!
Male researcher	Beauty might be the biggest mystery life has to offer, since there are few other topics commanding such strong emotions and beliefs among all of us. Mankind has never been able to agree on what is beautiful and what isn't and it seems we are drifting further apart as we speak. Almost every culture has its own, very specific ideas about what perfection looks like and celebrates its specific image of beauty. In our most recent research project, we have been trying to determine how realistic certain images and perceptions of beauty are. The expectations put forward by societies put pressure on both genders and have an especially far-reaching impact on young adults who – in most cases – have not yet established or finalised their own ideas on physical perfection. Since many societies have reached a point where they worship quite unnatural images of beauty which collide with reality, thousands of adolescents and young adults have to deal with the fact that they simply cannot achieve the aims they set for themselves. This growing gap between reality and expectations can be seen as responsible for a lack of self-confidence and pride in those age groups. When the images of physical perfection presented by the environment forces young men and women to despair due to the impossibility of reaching their goals, we risk destroying the vulnerable psyche of people who can no longer accept who they are. Apart from the unrealistic expectations towards people's physical appearances, there is another issue which we have been looking at in more detail. Beauty and its corresponding requirements are subject to constant change. Within a decade, most society's perceptions of beauty undergo several adjustments. While this has always been the case, the past decade has presented us with the most extreme variety of concepts. Since constant change commonly results in feelings of confusion and disorientation, people may even begin to suffer from psychological problems. The main problem lies in the fact that it is virtually impossible to withdraw from this vicious cycle, because there is no escaping the world surrounding us. If it was only fashion magazines and television shows, we might be able to distance ourselves from the ideas presented, but the message is there, in the clothes we buy, the packages our food is wrapped in, and the advertisements accompanying us throughout the day. Finally, there is one last aspect I think is worth mentioning. A growing number of people look for salvation in cosmetic surgery, hoping that a scalpel will achieve what all their efforts couldn't. However, what patients are commonly unaware of is that turning to cosmetic surgery is often only the first step to spinning out of control. Most people assume they will find peace after having undergone surgery. However, the truth often is that one operation leads to the next, because once we have perfected a small part of ourselves, our expectations increase and we start looking for the next part which could be corrected or improved.

▲50

▲50

3. Reading: Marriage between homosexual partners

Read the text below, then put the summarising statements (A–I) into the correct order. There are two extra summarising statements you should not use. Write your answers in the boxes provided. The first one (0) has been done for you.

Marriage between homosexual partners

Looking at the changes societal structures went through in recent years, it is not surprising that many people have a hard time adapting to new concepts and laws. While the fact that homosexual relationships exist and are acceptable seems to have sunk in, the idea of legalising marriages between same sex partners is far more critical in the eyes of its opponents.

One argument that is frequently coming up in discussion is the religious aspect of marriage. Since many religions do not accept homosexual relationships, they refuse to celebrate the bond between same sex partners in church and provide them with the possibility to speak their vows in a religious context. However, most homosexual couples do not strive for the church's tolerance but for legal appreciation of their decision to share their life.

When it comes to legal confirmation, opponents of legalising such marriages often claim that the protection and security such a legal bond offers should be reserved for heterosexual couples, who fulfil their image of proper couples. They argue that couples who are likely to raise families are in greater need of such protective laws and regulations than two adults who will never reproduce in a natural way.

Nevertheless, the question remains whether it would not violate basic human rights to refuse couples who fell in love the right to be partners also in a legal sense. This is especially true in reference to possible emergency situations, where homosexual partners often run into problems obtaining even the most basic information about each other from doctors or nurses when their partner has been hospitalised. In addition, people living together should also be able to inherit from each other or to perform other legal action possible for married couples.

However, opponents are often angered by the fact that such a legalisation might provide homosexual couples with financial benefits designed for couples willing to raise a family. In many countries married couples enjoy special forms of tax relief, which would then also be extended to same sex marriages. Nevertheless, this problem could easily be solved by introducing different tax regulations for any childless married couple, no matter whether it is homosexual or heterosexual.

The biggest concern, however, lies in the fact that childless married couples legally have the right to adopt children. If homosexual marriages were legalised, many opponents fear the partners would be eligible to apply for adoption. On the one hand, it is argued that

heterosexual couples who cannot naturally conceive should take priority over homosexual couples who made the decision to be with a partner they cannot naturally reproduce with. On the other hand, there is a conflict going on about whether children should be raised in a homosexual environment at all. Many of those presumptions, however, are driven by fear. There is no proof available that this way of raising children has any kind of negative effect on them. In the same spirit we could argue that any person with a habit that is not deemed acceptable or positive should not be allowed to reproduce. Nevertheless, these fears and prejudices towards homosexual couples are difficult to fight and are often rooted deep within the minds of people.

In order to increase tolerance and acceptance, it will be necessary to discuss this topic openly and honestly. By offering both opponents and supporters a platform to voice their concerns, we have the chance to make them understand and accept different points of view and we might actually reach our goal of treating people equally.

A	Homosexual couples are in a different situation, because they will not have any children.
B	Nowadays most people tend to tolerate homosexual relationships.
C	Not all legal actions possible for married couples should be open to same sex partners.
D	Homosexual couples aim for legal acceptance of their relationships.
E	The government would have to change the income laws for childless couples.
F	New laws would make the situation easier on hospital staff.
G	There are many prejudices against homosexual couples raising children.
H	Homosexual partners can't get married in any church.
I	Listening to different opinions about the issue could improve the situation.

KEY

0	Q1	Q2	Q3	Q4	Q5	Q6
B	D	A	F	E	G	I

4. Reading: The trouble with internships

Read the text below, then choose the correct heading (A–H) for each paragraph (1–5). There are two extra headings you should not use. Write your answers in the boxes provided at the end of the task. The first one (0) has been done for you.

The trouble with internships

... (0)

Lately most companies place more and more emphasis on work experience when hiring new staff. This, however, presents young people who have just finished their education with a huge problem, since even the best universities cannot provide them with the required practical knowledge. On realising that their chances to find employment are extremely slim without any experience, many people at the beginning of their career decide to enter an internship in order to gain knowledge on the job.

... (Q1)

Most companies do not mind hiring interns, because they provide an easy solution to the problem of covering peak times in production or service. Since especially larger companies have a need of interns, most of them offer similar types of internships. They are usually either not paid at all or present the workers with rather low wages. Additionally, such employment agreements are limited to a certain amount of time from the start and can also be terminated immediately from both parties. Most of these workers will work in assistance positions, since there is little time to train them for a job with higher responsibility. Although their duties resemble those of normal workers, their status does not require them to work independently.

... (Q2)

Before entering an internship, there are certain factors both parties, the employing company as well as the intern, have to clarify. Since firms may have varying work shifts and many interns are still finishing their education or have another job at the same time, both sides have to agree on possible work times. The workload may in many cases be less than that of a normal worker, although this has to be discussed in each individual case. In addition, many employers require proof of education or an impeccable reputation of the applicant

before hiring the intern. Only after making sure the requirements are met, a contract will be formed. Finally, signing non-disclosure clauses might be necessary in order to protect the company's product.

... (Q3)

Clearly internships have many possible benefits for young people. However, it is not always the case that such employment guarantees a job offer later on. Naturally many interns hope to be kept on by the company after a few months, but fail to realise that companies often have underlying reasons for employing interns that have nothing to do with later hiring. In addition, internships do not ensure that the worker gains experience in the area they are interested in or were aiming at. Finally, there is the question of income. The lack of payment for the work can cause major difficulties for interns.

... (Q4)

In the ideal case internships would simply be the perfect opportunity to first enter the job market. Once you have signed a contract for a position like that, it opens the door to making your first steps in a small or large company. Not always, however, does this decision prove to be a good one. As a matter of fact, interns work in relatively low positions, which often invite condescending behaviour of their superiors or even sexual harassment. Even if such incidents cannot be seen as normal occurrences, a raised awareness towards them might be necessary. Furthermore, the possibility of being used as a cheap worker instead of being instructed on appropriate work duties is a very real one.

... (Q5)

On the other hand, the assignments given to interns may be quite complex and challenging. Given that many people with internship contracts have received an excellent education, they are usually thought to be capable of performing certain high-skill duties, provided that they do not need any extra training on them. Same as normal workers, interns should do their jobs in the best way possible and be aware of the fact that they represent the company at any time. Being aware of this fact will help in succeeding during your internship.

▼54

▼53

ōbv © Österreichischer Bundesverlag Schulbuch GmbH & Co. KG, Wien 2014 | Alle Rechte vorbehalten | www.oebv.at | www.testen-und-foerdern.at
Prime Time 8. Testen und Fördern, Arbeitsheft (ISBN 978-3-209-08444-6)

5. Language in use: The significance of being different

You are going to read a text about the significance of being different. In most lines of the text there is a word that should not be there. Write that word in the space provided after each line. Seven to nine lines are correct. Indicate these lines with a tick (✓). There are two examples at the beginning.

The significance of being different

Younger generations have always aimed at being as different from the
generations before them, mostly because they commonly feel the need to
establish their own style, identity, and way of life. The result is a huge gap
between older and younger members of society, which in the turn causes
major conflicts and frequent disagreements.
Another consequence out of this fact is the perception of younger people
as to being disrespectful and ungrateful towards their elders, even though
most young adults' efforts to be different rather originate in their desire to
create something new than in their wish to overthrow what others will
have worked for or to rebel against anything and anybody.
However, among of members of one generation the basic ideals and
expectations on life are normally quite so similar. Up until now most
people belonging to a specific age of group tended to display certain
types of hairstyle, clothes, and behaviour. Nevertheless, the members of
recent generations show a tendency towards the placing an increased
importance on being individuals who differ from each and other. This rise
in individualism is especially noticeable when it comes to the way people
behave in society, which is becoming increasingly extrovert and outspoken.

KEY

0	as
00	✓
Q1	the
Q2	✓
Q3	✓
Q4	out
Q5	to
Q6	✓
Q7	will
Q8	✓
Q9	of
Q10	so
Q11	of
Q12	✓
Q13	the
Q14	and
Q15	✓
Q16	✓

A	Drawbacks of internships
B	The new-found importance of internships
C	Laws for internships
D	Risks of entering such types of employment
E	Common similarities of internships
F	Possible consequences of internships
G	Expectations on interns
H	Agreements between interns and companies

KEY

0	Q1	Q2	Q3	Q4	Q5
B	H	A	D	G	

6. Language in use: Successful businessmen and -women

You are going to read a text about businesspeople. Some words are missing from the text. Fill in the word which best fits each gap (1–7). Use only one word in each gap. Write your answers in the spaces provided at the end of the text. The first one (0) has been done for you.

Successful businessmen and -women

Most successful businessmen and -women are well aware **(0)** … the envy they are constantly met with. It is no secret that most of us see wealth, power and influence as something to aspire to. Nevertheless, most people on top of the food **(Q1)** … did not simply reap the benefits of their parents' lifelong work, but put endless hours into **(Q2)** … their set goals. They know that it is hard work to stay where they are at and that one tiny mistake can be the cause of their downfall.

In **(Q3)** … to become a successful manager, there are certain character traits you should possess. To begin with, you have to be dedicated to your profession and willing to learn every little aspect of it. The more you know about the individual aspects of your company or department, **(Q4)** … more likely it is that you make informed and useful decisions. In addition, knowledge about marketing **(Q5)** … economic principles, and accounting is necessary to ensure you are doing a good job as a manager.

Naturally, there are many benefits to pursuing a successful career. Once you have made it, there are rewards far **(Q6)** … what most other people receive for doing their jobs. Nevertheless, the risks you take are equally extreme, since businessmen and -women rank among the groups with the highest risk of burn out or depression and suffering **(Q7)** … physical symptoms of stress, such as ulcers.

KEY

0	of
Q1	chain
Q2	achieving, reaching
Q3	order
Q4	the
Q5	strategies, methods
Q6	beyond
Q7	from

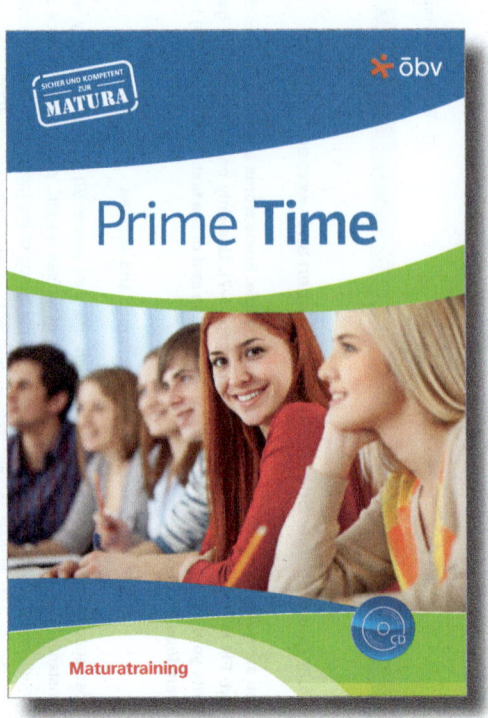

Georg Hellmayr, Stephan Waba

Prime Time
Maturatraining

64 Seiten, A4
ISBN 978-3-209-07404-1

Die optimale Vorbereitung auf die Standardisierte Reifeprüfung

- **Drei komplette Probematuren**
- **Maturatraining für Lesen, Hören, Sprachverwendung im Kontext, Schreiben und Sprechen**
- **Alle Übungen in den neuen österreichischen Testformaten**
- **Beigelegte CD mit Hörtexten, Tapescripts und allen Lösungen**

Direkt beim Verlag (www.oebv.at) bestellbar oder im Buchhandel erhältlich.
Österreichischer Bundesverlag Schulbuch GmbH & Co. KG
www.oebv.at, Telefon 01 · 401 36 - 36